C000156374

The Splendid Shilling

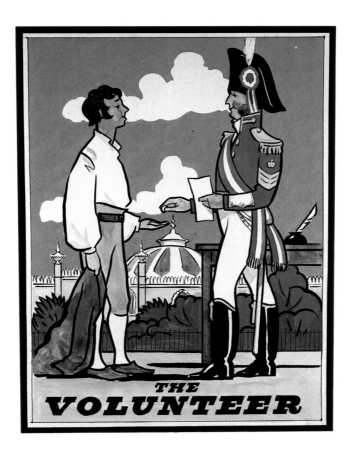

THE SHILLING ENLISTS A RECRUIT
Accepting a shilling was meant to symbolize a youth's enlistment into military service, but it came to be abused by over-zealous recruiting officers who sometimes proffered free drinks. Public houses provided glass-bottomed mugs so that the shillings placed there by recruiting sergeants could be spotted. The custom of passing over "earnest-money" was discontinued in the reign of Queen Victoria (see Chapter XIV). Shown above is the inn sign of "The Volunteer" in Brighton.

The Splendid Shilling

A Social History of an Engaging Coin

JAMES O'DONALD MAYS

"Happy the man, who void of cares and strife
In silken or leathern purse retains
A splendid shilling."
John Phillips (1676–1709)

NEW FOREST LEAVES
Burley, Ringwood, Hampshire

© James O'Donald Mays 1982

All rights reserved. No part of this publication may be reproduced, stored in a retrieval system, or transmitted in any form or by any means (electronic, mechanical, photocopying, recording or otherwise) without the prior permission of the copyright owner.

British Library Cataloguing in Publication Data:

Mays, James O'Donald
  The Splendid Shilling: The Social History of an Engaging Coin.
  1. Shilling – History
  I. Title
  332.4′042   HG555
  ISBN 0-907956-00-9

Set in 10/11 Baskerville by Pintail Studios Limited,
and printed in Great Britain by Pardy & Son (Printers) Limited,
both of Ringwood, Hampshire,
for New Forest Leaves, Burley, Ringwood, Hampshire

For
ANGELA

Contents

Acknowledgements

Illustrations comprise a substantial portion of this work and the author wishes to express his gratitude to the following institutions and individuals for providing them (on the pages indicated): Ashmolean Museum 18, 21, 25, 31, 33, 35, 36, 40, 41, 43, 46, 48, 49, 50, 52, 54, 57, 59, 60, 64, 67, 69, 70, 71, 73, 77, 79, 82, 83, 87, 96, 97, 99, 103, 104, 105, 106, 110, 113, 115, 124, 215; Australian High Commission 135; Avon County Library (Braikenridge Collection) 27, 68; Bermuda Department of Tourism 128, 129; Birmingham Public Libraries (Local Studies Department) 92; Bodleian Library 7, 48; the Trustees of the British Museum 23, 32, 34, 36, 55, 56, 74, 75, 81, 83, 118, 119, 120, 121, 130, 132, 133; British Tourist Authority 44, 66, 81, 115, 158; Commonwealth of Virginia (The Jamestown–Yorktown Foundation) 13; *Country Life* 80; *Everywoman's Encyclopedia* 10; Nicholas Gossip 139; Tom Hanley (Australian Numismatic Society) 94; Miss F. Hardcastle 148; Controller of Her Majesty's Stationery Office (Crown Copyright) 19, 109, 111; Terry Hood-Cree 150, 162, 168; National Museum of Antiquities of Scotland 126; National Portrait Gallery 24, 26, 30, 35, 40, 52, 57, 61, 63, 70, 73, 77, 79, 97, 99, 103, 106, 113; National Trust 28; New Zealand High Commission 136; J. J. North and Spink & Son, Ltd. 42; His Grace the Duke of Northumberland 80; Peter Parkinson 91, 92; The Pilgrim Press, Ltd. frontispiece; *Punch* 65, 101; Royal Commonwealth Society 109; Royal National Museum, Copenhagen 17; The Scout Association and British Leyland 11; Seaby, Ltd. 19; The Royal Coin Cabinet, Stockholm 17; Uganda High Commission (R. S. M. Ibreck) 139; United States Navy 114; University of Oslo (Coin Cabinet) 17; Frederick Warne 159; Keith Waterton 17, 134, 135, 136, 137, 138, 139, 140, 142, 143; Mrs. S. Watney 9, 102; Watneys Southern for the jacket and frontispiece illustration of the inn sign of "The Volunteer" at Brighton, taken from a preliminary design by the late Southby Bramwell; West Sussex Record Office by kind permission of Mrs. P. Gill, County Archivist 87.

For quotations and references in the text the author is indebted to The American Numismatic Society for background on early American shillings; Professor John Burnett, Brunel University, for permission to quote from his *A History of the Cost of Living* (Penguin Books, 1969); Dr. Christopher Challis, University of Leeds, for background on some Tudor coins; Methuen & Co. and A. P. Watt Ltd. for permission to use excerpts from "Shillin' A Day" by Rudyard Kipling from his *Barrack Room Ballads*; Her Majesty's Stationery Office for use of Crown Copyright material taken from *The Proposed Coinage of King Edward VIII*, by G. P. Dyer, taken from the report of the Deputy Master and Controller of The Royal Mint; the Ministry of Defence Library for background on the use of the shilling in military recruitment; The Law Society for references to the shilling used in wills; The Scout Association for the history of the Bob-a-Job institution; Tom Hanley for background on the shilling token of Tasmania; C. N. Popper of The Shilling Coffee Co. for aspects of his firm's history; Miss F. Hardcastle for permission to quote from various historical references; Frederick Warne, Ltd., for permission to quote (and use the illustration) from Edward Lear's *Nonsense Omnibus*; the following for background on the skillings of Scandinavia: Jørgen Steen Jensen, Royal National Museum, Copenhagen; Kenneth Jonsson, Royal Coin Cabinet, Stockholm; Jan H. Nordbø, Coin Cabinet, University of Oslo; The Austrian State Mint for background on the Austrian schilling; the Reference Librarians of Brighton, Bristol, Carlisle, Ringwood and Scarborough for supplying numismatic references of one kind or another; the Guildhall Library, City of London, for the account of Christ's Hospital scholars and The Lord Mayor's shilling; and J. M. Dent & Sons, Ltd., for permission to reproduce "The Adventures of the Shilling" from their Everyman's Library edition of *The Tatler*.

Appreciation is also due those scholars who have provided assistance or suggestions in specific areas; these include Arthur Blair, Peter A. Clayton, Michael Dolley, Patrick Finn, Nicholas Mayhew, Major T. K. R. Murray, W. A. Seaby and A. E. J. Went. For reading sizeable portions of the manuscript in various stages of preparation, the author is grateful to Dr. John Kent, Howard Linecar, Robert H. Thompson, and Dr. Phillip Whitting.

It is impossible to thank sufficiently two scholars who made many suggestions over a period of years for improving or adding to the content; without their assistance and encouragement the work would not have been possible in its present form. They are S. R. Denny and G. P. Dyer, Librarian and Curator of The Royal Mint.

Space does not permit mention of others who have assisted either the research or production stages of the book. Having thanked those who made substantial contributions to the work, the author emphasizes that any errors or omissions are his own; if they can be brought to his attention, they will be rectified in any future edition.

Finally, a word of appreciation is due the firm of M. R. Taylor for their unfailing understanding and courtesy during the research stage of the work, and to Anton Cox, production manager of Pardy and Son, whose sensitive approach to technical considerations has materially affected the appearance of this volume.

Preface

Why, the reader may ask, a social history of the shilling?

The answer, it seems to me, must surely lie in the uniqueness of the shilling. It alone, among the thousands of coins issued in the civilized world, has surrounded itself with such a body of historical, economic and literary associations as to merit individual treatment in book form.

A social history is supposed to be history without heavy reliance on political events. In the case of the shilling it has been impossible to ignore either political or economic conditions, for it has always been the coin of the people. As such, it became on occasion a propaganda device for zealous rulers, and always was a barometer of the times in which it passed from hand to hand. But in the main, I have attempted to show how this coin has endeared itself to generations of people – in Britain, in America and in the Commonwealth – through events and associations involving monarchs and their subjects, priests and pirates, and the rich and poor. In short, the shilling was Everyman's coin.

Naturally, the purchasing power of the shilling and its talismanic role with the public has changed with the times. In the Tudor period, when it was the favoured piece for popular shove-board games, it could be a week's wages. In the reign of Queen Elizabeth II it still had considerable purchasing power. It would buy a daily newspaper, several boxes of matches and would prepay the cost of sendin a letter within the United Kingdom. Up until it was replaced by the five penny coin, it remained the denomination most seized upon for usefulness – and for casual reference – in everyday life.

The shilling's story is not confined to Britain. In Stuart times it crossed the Atlantic to North America where it circulated in Bermuda, Massachusetts and New England, and Maryland. Later it appeared in other areas where there was a British presence: Australia, New Zealand, East Africa, South Africa, West Africa, Rhodesia, Cyprus, Fiji and New Guinea. Ireland had her own shillings from the Tudor period to the recent decimalization. When the wave of nationalism swept across Africa in the 1960s, a host of new countries continued with the shilling and some have retained it to this day.

The general reader, for whom this book is primarily intended, will find very few numismatic terms have been used. The most common of these is "obverse" which simply means that side of a coin portraying the monarch or other leader, and usually bearing the name of the issuing country. The specialist, on the other hand, will find that virtually every major variety of shilling is to be found among the 130 pieces illustrated and described. I have not included patterns or trial pieces, with the notable exceptions of the very first shilling, Henry VII's testoon, and the shilling of Edward VIII.

The work ends with three essays, one each being taken from the eighteenth, nineteenth and twentieth centuries. Its great length precluded the reproduction of John Taylor's "A Shilling or, The Travailes of Twelve-Pence;" otherwise, the seventeenth century would have been added to the group of literary works chronicling the shilling's adventures.

Despite my attempt to include varied references to the shilling, both anecdotal and literary, I am sure there must be others that have escaped my notice. If readers know of other such associations – whether of British or other origin – I would be pleased to hear of them.

Finally, it is my hope that anyone possessing a shilling, whether of recent or ancient issue, may through these pages savour something of the times in which it circulated, and perhaps ponder upon the joy or sadness it brought each successive holder.

J.O.M.

I
Introduction: A Coin of Convenience

"THE LAND OF WILLIAM OF BRAIOSE. In REDINGES hundred. . . . There is a mill of 18 shillings-worth and a fishery of 50 pence-worth. It [the estate] was worth £4; now [it is worth] 100 shillings."

Extract from the Domesday Book.

Although the shilling did not exist as an actual coin until the reign of Henry VII, it was in use long before that time as a unit of value, or reckoning. Pounds, shillings and pence were used (along with the mark – valued at 13s 4d) in Saxon times whenever it became necessary to value farm animals offered for sale, calculate wages or board, or sell land or property.

During the reign of King Athelstan (922–940) a sheep, by the laws of the sovereign, was valued at a shilling.[1] Interestingly, the fleece of the sheep was estimated as being about two-fifths of the value of the animal. A cow was valued at four times the worth of a sheep, and an ox six times. During the tenth century land cost just above a shilling an acre. Thus it will be seen that the shilling, as a kind of yardstick for everyday commerce, was already established as the most important, or cardinal value in everyday English life.

When the first of the Norman rulers ascended the English throne, the shilling was still firmly established as the unit that was used most often in transactions by the average citizen. William I, fearing an invasion by King Canute of Denmark, levied a tax of six shillings on every "hide" – the term given a parcel of land deemed sufficient to support a family of average size. Shortly thereafter, to help determine his fiscal rights and establish a basis for taxation, he ordered a comprehensive survey of the nation's resources. The result of this gigantic inventory, the Domesday Book, reveals that the shilling – along with some other denominations – was firmly established as a unit for reckoning the value of houses, animals, mills, land and other assets.

Over 600 Bricks for a Shilling

As England moved into the Middle Ages, the shilling continued to feature prominently in the costing of articles of everyday use.[2] During the 13th century a shilling would buy a pair of shoes, and land could be bought for seven shillings an acre. Bricks were cheap at a shilling for 660, or 1/6 per 1,000. It is estimated, at this price, that Eton College probably cost no more than £75 to build. The cost of food in medieval times was also low. A shilling would buy a sheep, its value having remained unchanged since pre-Norman days. Pigs were 3/6 each, and an ox 9s. Sugar varied between a shilling and two shillings a pound, but a shilling went a long way toward supplying a family's stock of spices and exotic foods. Pepper hovered around a shilling a pound; ginger ranged from just below a shilling a pound to as much as 2/6. A shilling would purchase five pounds of almonds and two luscious pomegranates. In contrast to these bargains, a young scholar attending Oxford was apt to regard the university's fines as exorbitant. For threats of personal assault, he was fined the princely sum of a shilling.

DOOMSDAY BOOK *presented to* WILL.™ 1.

THE DOMESDAY BOOK

This survey of England, dating from the reign of William the Conqueror, makes many mentions of the shilling as a unit of account. In this old print, the Domesday Book is being presented to William I.

With the advent of the Tudors, England moved into an age of expansion – both at home and abroad. The shilling, a unit of accounting up to now, was at last struck as a coin of the realm. It could buy substantial amounts of food and clothing. Toward the end of the reign of Henry VIII a shilling would buy nearly two bushels of wheat, and an artisan could earn up to 4s a week in wages.

But England – for centuries an agrarian society with a slowly growing population – now began to experience dramatic upheaval as the price for its emergence as a world power. Inflation rose sharply, but wages did not always keep pace with the sharp increase in prices of goods. Economists who assigned a base figure of 100 at the start of Henry VIII's reign estimate the cost of living had risen to 470 on James I's accession, and 557 by the time of the Civil Wars. Yet, despite this inflation and the uncertainties of the wars, a shilling could still buy a great deal. The Earl of Bedford paid a shilling for a lobster in 1660, and a few years later a shilling would also buy three pounds of rice, two bottles of cider, or a pint of sack. However primitive the operation may have been in Stuart times, extracting a tooth was a bargain at a shilling.

For most of the 18th century a shilling a day was considered good pay for all except the highly skilled. Farm workers and the unskilled received slightly less. By the mid-1700s the cost of living was eight times what it was under the Tudors. Surprisingly, the shilling was still a welcome coin on market day. It could purchase 5 lbs. of meat or four rabbits, 3 quarts of strong ale, or 6 gallons of "middling" beer. The coin would also allow the traveller to ride about 4 miles on the stagecoach in winter, and a slightly greater distance in summer. At a noted Liverpool inn, "The Lion," a couple could pay a shilling and enjoy a fine meal consisting of veal cutlets, pigeons, asparagus, lamb and salad, apple-pie and tarts. In London

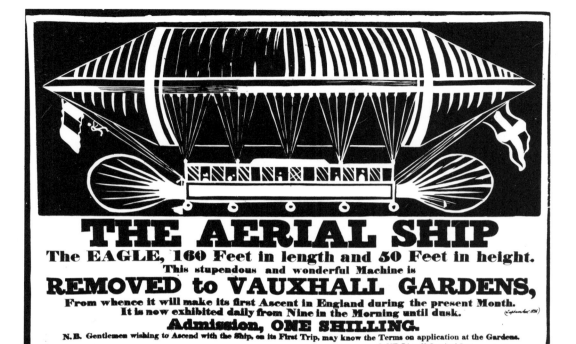

THE AERIAL SHIP
The EAGLE, 160 Feet in length and 50 Feet in height.
This stupendous and wonderful Machine is
REMOVED to VAUXHALL GARDENS,
From whence it will make its first Ascent in England during the present Month.
It is now exhibited daily from Nine in the Morning until dusk. *(September 1835)*
Admission, ONE SHILLING.
N.B. Gentlemen wishing to Ascend with the Ship, on its First Trip, may know the Terms on application at the Gardens.
BALNE, Printer, 38, Gracechurch Street.

A SHILLING'S WORTH OF EXCITEMENT IN VAUXHALL

A "stupendous and wonderful machine" in London's Vauxhall Gardens could be viewed for only a shilling in September, 1835. For those courageous gentlemen wishing to ascend in the aerial ship, the price was undoubtedly more.

the shilling had a slightly lower purchasing power than in the provinces, but nonetheless went a long way in supplying items for the family larder. For twelve pence one could get almost 4 lbs. of meat, $1\frac{1}{2}$ lbs. of salt butter, almost 3 oz. of tea, 2 lbs. of sugar, and 2 lbs. of cheese.

The 19th century saw Britain become an industrialized nation. Stage coaches were still popular and rides were cheap. In 1816 an inside passenger on the Liverpool–Lancaster stagecoach run had to pay 7s., while the hardier (or less well-off) passenger sitting outside paid only a 5s. fare. In the cities omnibuses were bargains. A shilling would take a passenger about five miles – sometimes farther. It would buy a ticket from Brentford to St. Paul's, or from Richmond to the centre of London. Early rail fares were about the same: a shilling for approximately five miles.

Although the shilling still had much purchasing power, it was not that easy to come by for the poor. William Cobbett, writing of a visit to Durley, Hampshire, in 1823, with "Farmer Mears" and his family, was astonished to learn that the two daughters of the farmer earned as much as their father by plaiting straw. "They had made a plat of several degrees of fineness," he noted, "and they sell it to some person or persons, at Fareham, who

I suppose, makes it into bonnets. Each of the girls earns, per week, as much (within a shilling) as her father, who is a labouring man. The father has at this time only 7/- a week. Thus the income of the family is raised to 19/- a week."[3]

40 Cigarettes for a Shilling

The dawn of the 20th century brought a welcome drop in the price of some household needs. A shilling would now buy a full pound of coffee, 6 lbs. of soap, and a dozen candles. It would also purchase six tablespoons for the family table. In the reign of Edward VII a shilling would provide the smoker with no less than 40 cigarettes and the gourmet with a dozen fine oysters. During this same reign income tax was raised from a shilling in the pound to the 'staggering" rate of 1s 2d in the pound, an increase which was roundly condemned by the press of the day as "plundering of the middle class."

Diarists throughout the ages have referred to the prices they paid for food, or a night's lodging as they traversed these lovely isles. None perhaps has described these travels so vividly, and the cost of their meals and accommodation with such frankness as Samuel Pepys. A typical entry in his diary, one in which the shilling figured prominently, is that for June 11th, 1668, when he was in Salisbury. Pepys found the George Inn pleasant enough ("a silk bed; and very good diet") but was annoyed when the inn could not provide coach-horses for his planned journey to Stonehenge. Instead, he and his party were obliged to accept saddle-horses, which Pepys found "very dear." Following the visit to Stonehenge's circle of giant stones ("God knows what their use was!"), Pepys returned to the George Inn in time for dinner. ". . . that being done," he wrote in his diary, " [I] paid the reckoning, which was so exorbitant and particular in rate of my horses, and 7s. 6d. for bread and beer, that I was mad, and resolve[d] to trouble the master about it, and get something for the poor; and came away in that humour; L2:5:6. Servants, 1s.6.d.; poor, 1s; guide to the Stones, 2s.; poor woman in the street, 1s; . . . washerwoman, 1/s. . . . ."[4]

Apart from its role for more than four and a half centuries as a coin of convenience, the shilling often has found itself useful for its size in measuring things or simply as a talisman for bringing good luck. Many such employments of the shilling have occurred within living memory, and a few still remain with us.

Joseph Addison, writing in *The Spectator* in 1711, recorded one of the earliest mentions of the shilling as a love token. "Among the several ways of Consolation which absent Lovers make use of while their Souls are in that State of Departure, which, you say, is Death in Love," he wrote, ". . . the First and Foremost is a crooked shilling, which has administered great comfort to our Fore-fathers, and is still made use of on this Occasion with very good Effect in most Parts of Her Majesty's Dominions . . . ."[5] No one knows who bent the first shilling or how many lonely maidens have gained solace through gazing upon their crooked shillings, but the custom of giving love tokens was followed as recently as the Second World War.

An Unusual Use of the Shilling: a Coin of Persuasion

In bygone times the shilling was employed to move certain people on their way, usually against their will. Discharged servicemen and others would wander about the countryside, halting and taking up temporary residence in this or that village to which they took a liking. They were perfectly aware, if they remained long enough, that they would become public charges. Hence villagers were alert to these "visitors" and as soon as their purpose was detected, tried to move them on. Oral persuasion, however, often was not enough. Old

"A KNIFE, A SHILLING AND A PIECE OF STRING"

These were the three essentials for anyone starting out into the countryside in the days when horse-drawn transport was the principal means of getting about. The shilling was the accepted sum for a gratuity when assistance was needed.

records of the village of Burley in the New Forest record, after the Napoleonic Wars, that two destitute seamen – about to become charges of the parish – agreed to depart when presented with a shilling each.[6] This was common practice throughout the land.

More recently, the shilling has been helpful in "moving" people, but in quite different circumstances from the above. When horse-drawn transport was the universal means of getting around, a sensible driver had to be prepared for unexpected problems. He was wise if he followed an old admonition to take along "A knife, a string, and a shilling."[7] The knife was for cutting the harness, when required, and for removing stones from the hoof; the string was for mending broken reins; and the shilling was a useful gratuity for the assistance which inevitably would be required.

The Shilling as a Tool

Of all the uses of the shilling perhaps few are so clever as those in which the coin is employed as an actual instrument for measuring, or as a pattern for needlework. An 1857

RECALLING RUSKIN'S "MAJESTY OF ORDERED LINES"
This needlework pattern of a briar rose was made by tracing round a shilling; it
appeared two generations ago in the popular *Everywoman's Encyclopedia*.

recipe for egg balls dispenses with measuring spoons, weights or whatever, and simply
states that the cook should use as much salt as will life flat upon a shilling.

Early in the reign of George V a delightful set of books found their way into many British
homes. Entitled *Everywoman's Encyclopedia*, they sought to provide information and
entertainment exclusively for women. The charm of the essays in this set of volumes, and
the range of subjects covered, probably has not been exceeded by any modern publishing
enterprise aimed at the feminine reader. One essay entitled "Making Patterns with Coins,"
was written especially for needleworkers "who cannot draw correct curves, as well as those
who can but . . . love to exercise their ingenuity . . .." Of several designs presented, that of
the briar rose made from a shilling is perhaps the most exquisite. "A shilling made the
design," the author of the essay says, "or, rather, the act of tracing round this useful coin,
stiffened those circles into beauty, and made what Ruskin rightly calls 'the majesty of
ordered lines.' "[8]

Mintage Figures for the Shilling

Perhaps the most authentic means of indicating the shilling's popularity since 1816, when
reliable Mint records begin, is that of comparing the number of coins struck in this
denomination with figures for other silver values. Of the 147 years since 1816 when silver
pieces were issued, the shilling topped the mintage tables for 70 years, followed by the
sixpence with 54 years. In Queen Victoria's reign, the shilling was particularly in demand:
the numbers struck led other denominations combined by 43 to 21 years, and for one 12-
year period (1864–75) it led the list.

Bob-a-Job

The shilling became a symbol of hard work shortly after the Second World War when it
was adopted by Boy Scouts as the minimum payment hoped for in their annual Bob-a-Job
Week. It was Lord Baden-Powell himself who first developed the concept of a work day. In
1914 when funds were badly needed to provide literature in Braille for the blind, he invited
Boy Scouts to let themselves out for hire on a particular day. Thirty years later Haydn
Dimmock borrowed the work-day notion of Lord Baden-Powell's, extended the period of

"BOB A JOB" – A NATIONAL SCOUTING INSTITUTION

For an entire generation Scouts in virtually every community in Britain have undertaken small tasks during the annual Scout Job Week. The suggested payment for these jobs was a shilling and "Bob A Job" became a familiar by-word up and down the land. Even with the advent of decimalization and super-inflation, the term continues to be used by a large segment of the public. In the photograph above a group of Scouts tackle a dirty car.

work to a week and added the suggested shilling payment. By 1949 the scheme had caught on all over Britain and it has thrived ever since, earning hundreds of thousands of pounds for local Scout groups and the national office. When the shilling was decimalized in 1970, the name of the annual event was changed to "Scout Job Week."

Shilling Bargains

At one time or another in the last two centuries, the shilling represented such a bargain that its very name became incorporated with the item purchased. Perhaps the most common of these were in the realm of literature where many works sold for a shilling. Some titles,

Announcement of a High-class Pictorial Guide *to the* Midland Railway.

Messrs. CASSELL, PETTER, GALPIN & CO. have much pleasure in announcing that they have concluded arrangements with the Midland Railway Company for the production and publication of

The Official Illustrated Guide to the Midland Railway.

About 400 pages 8vo, price **1s.**

IN this Guide will be described the Picturesque Scenery and Places of Interest on the entire system of the Midland Railway, extending over upwards of *Twelve Hundred Miles* of the fairest Scenery in the Kingdom. It will be enriched with HIGH-CLASS ENGRAVINGS on nearly every page, and will, moreover, contain a complete series of ROUTE MAPS, in which will be found delineated each notable object to be seen from the carriage window or adjacent to the line, and Sectional BIRD'S-EYE VIEW MAPS, printed in Colours, indicating the whole country east and west of the Midland Railway, with the natural features—lakes, rivers, mountain chains, &c. &c.

Prospectuses will be sent post free on application, and Orders are now received by all Booksellers and at the Railway Bookstalls.

CASSELL, PETTER, GALPIN & Co., LUDGATE HILL, LONDON.

A 400-PAGE ILLUSTRATED GUIDE FOR ONLY A SHILLING
As railway enthusiasts will appreciate, the announcement a century ago of this guide to the Midland Railway line was regarded as a great publication event.

indeed, were classics of the language, but others were tales of adventure and romance. These latter, rich "cousins" of "Penny Dreadfuls," came to be known as "Shilling Shockers." Most publishers had a long list of books which sold for a shilling, including popular reference works. One such, sold by Cassells, was to be found in thousands of kitchens – the indispensable *Shilling Cookery Book*. Music lovers, too, were pleased that famous musical compositions – Handel's "Messiah," for example – sold for a shilling a copy. As recently as 1938 the shilling could still buy a pound of coffee at a respected London firm which assumed the coin's name. The firm's founder was an ingenious trader who conceived the notion of selling coffee directly to the public at a price per pound (a shilling) which was a considerable bargain.[9] This firm, incidentally, prepaid the postage (only 1s. 1d.) if one bought 14 lbs. of coffee; when the shilling gave way to its decimal equivalent in 1970, it would prepay only the cost of a letter.

The Shilling in Two Decimal Coinage Attempts

Commissioners appointed to study the advisability of decimal coinage for Britain pointed to the shilling as the most convenient of the coin of the realm. In 1859 their final report argued that the pound should be the principal unit in any proposed decimal coinage for the country, but went on to say that the shilling was undoubtedly "the leading *coin*" (italics are the author's). The reason for the endorsement of the shilling's role was an entirely practical one: "the most convenient size for a coin in which considerable, but not very large, sums are

REPLICAS OF THREE FAMOUS SHIPS AT JAMESTOWN, VIRGINIA
In May, 1607, three ships – the SUSAN CONSTANT, GODSPEED, and
DISCOVERY – brought 105 English colonists to present-day Virginia. In 1956
replicas of the three vessels (pictured above) were built in England as part of the
350th anniversary celebration of Jamestown as America's first permanent settlement. When the ships were handed over, the American ambassador was presented
with newly struck shillings of James I and Queen Elizabeth II in keeping with the
tradition of placing coins of the realm beneath construction.

to be paid, is the smallest size which can be conveniently taken up between the finger and
thumb and counted."[10]

More than 60 years later, in 1920, another commission reported on its findings after a
similar study on decimalization. This time the body recommended that the shilling, not the
pound, be adopted as the basic unit of decimal coinage and that it be divided into 100 parts.
The Commission received reports from Chambers of Commerce throughout Britain, and
most regarded the shilling as the nation's most useful coin.[11] The Newcastle–Gateshead
Chamber pointed out that before the First World War the penny had been the most
favoured coin of the poor, but during the war the shilling had become the piece most frequently employed by them. But adopting decimal coinage was a bold move, and it was not
to be until 1971 that Britain would officially adopt the system.

Shillings to Virginia

The shilling coin was barely a hundred years old when English colonists settled in Virginia.
James I was on the throne at the time (1607) and this first permanent English settlement

was duly named "Jamestown" after him. In 1956 the state of Virginia was making elaborate preparations to mark the 350th anniversary of Jamestown in the following year. One of the many projects planned to celebrate the anniversary was the construction in England of exact-scale replicas of the three vessels which had brought the original settlers to Virginia. On completion, the ships were to sail to Virginia.

By modern standards, the vessels were extremely small. The largest of the three, the "Susan Constant," was a "giant" of one hundred tons; the "Godspeed" was forty tons and the smallest ship, the 'Discovery," was only twenty tons. Just as proud builders of houses in bygone days sometimes placed current coins of the realm in fireplaces, and civic leaders put shiny new coins in the foundation stones of public buildings, so it was the custom in former times to place shillings of the reign beneath the masts of sailing ships being constructed.

So that the building of the "Susan Constant," the "Godspeed," and the "Discovery" could conform to this ancient tradition, the Royal Mint made a rare departure from its principle of not allowing old coin dies to be used again. On this occasion permission was granted for striking seven shillings from dies of the reign of James I. These, together with seven shillings of Queen Elizabeth II, were presented to the United States Ambassador in a ceremony at 11 Downing Street. The Chancellor of the Exchequer, in his capacity as Master of the Mint, presided over the presentation.[12]

It was thus singularly appropriate that the shilling, this time as a talisman of Anglo-American relations, should be the centre of attention during the last reign under which it would circulate in its own name.

Let us now examine in detail the "adventures" which befell this coin of convenience through the centuries.

The Coins

II
Out of the Dark Came the Shilling

"Let me design its coins and I do not care who writes the history of my country."
An anonymous author writing in *The Numismatic Review*, June 1943.

Although the term "shilling" is not of British origin, scholars are unsure of its exact derivation. One school of thought suggests the word comes from the Latin *siliqua*, which came to be a small coin – the twenty-fourth part of a solidus. Others take the view that the term has Teutonic origins, possibly deriving from *skell* (to resound or to ring), or *skel* (sometimes spelled *skil*), meaning "to divide."[1] Most scholars lean toward a Teutonic origin and point out that early references to the shilling (sometimes spelled "scilling") suggest a rough "coin" which could be easily divided into small portions.

In the Anglo-Saxon poem "Widsith" there was a king of the Goths who presented a gift of "an armlet of six hundred pieces of beaten gold scored, in scillings reckoned." This interesting reference suggests an armlet made of gold with scoring marks at regular intervals and which, like modern cakes of chocolate, could be broken off, bit by bit, as desired. Thus a sale could necessitate breaking off two bits of metal, or whatever number was needed. Eventually the armlet would no longer be an armlet, and merely a piece of detachable coin.

Continental Schillings and Skillings

On the continent of Europe the shilling, spelled variously as *schilling* in Germanic countries and *skilling* in Scandinavia, also was in use, first as a money of account and later as a coin. Toward the beginning of the 15th century a host of mints – among them Lubeck, Hamburg, Stuttgart, Wurtemburg, Augsburg, Wismar and others in Prussia and Livonia (present-day Latvia) – issued schillings. The Scandinavian skillings appeared considerably later, those of Denmark struck in the reign of Christopher of Bavaria during the 1440s being the first. Norway issued skillings in 1515 and Sweden not until 1777. By 1875 the Scandinavian skillings had disappeared; those struck for the Danish West Indies ceased even earlier (1859). After a hiatus of half a century, a continental schilling reappeared in 1924 when Austria issued an attractive silver piece depicting its parliament building. Austria remains the only continental nation where the schilling is still a denomination. The fortunes of the shilling in Britain, on the other hand, were not so erratic as those of its continental namesake. Once established here as an actual coin, it was to remain so until the reign of Elizabeth II.

Nonetheless, the advent of the English shilling was profoundly influenced by events in Europe. With Henry Tudor's victory over Richard III on Bosworth Field, England moved from the Middle Ages into an era of renaissance and progress. All Europe was experiencing a great awakening and England, though late to be roused, was not to be left out of it. The arts flourished with numerous works of outstanding beauty and realism. Printing by movable type developed and by the end of Henry VII's reign some four hundred titles had been published in England.

SOME SHILLINGS OF THE CONTINENT

A GERMAN SCHILLING

Certain German cities and provinces issued *schillings*, some before Britain's first shilling was struck. Shown here is a relatively modern (1767) Mecklenberg schilling.

DANISH SKILLING

In Denmark the *skilling* circulated for four centuries, but is now an obsolete denomination.

A NORWEGIAN SKILLING

This *skilling*, issued in 1870, appeared when Norway was united with Sweden but nonetheless had its own coinage.

SWEDEN'S KING

Charles XIV is shown on this Swedish *skilling* of 1832. Sweden's familiar three crowns appear on the reverse.

AUSTRIAN SCHILLING

This *schilling* of 1925 depicts the Parliament. Austria is the only nation in Europe to retain the schilling or a variation of it, as a coin.

COINS OF THE RENAISSANCE	**TESTOON'S REVERSE**
The exquisite *testone* of the Duke of Milan (left) may well have inspired the designer of Henry VII's testoon (right). The Milan piece was struck during 1481–94, and the English testoon in about 1504.	Henry VII's testoon bears a simple quartered shield device encircled by a religious legend. Note the French fleur-de-lys.

Henry, the first of the Tudors, was determined that his people should share in the new spirit which was sweeping over Western Europe. He had gained his crown by the sword, but desired to keep his country at peace, both at home and with her neighbours on the continent. In a master stroke of strategy, he dissolved the rivalry between the Yorkists and the Lancastrians by marrying Elizabeth of York. Henry was an efficient ruler and even took the trouble to countersign pages in his accountant's books.

Henry VII's Testoon – the First English Shilling

Through his contact with European royalty, Henry was able to keep abreast of contemporary trends in the fine arts – including that of portraiture. A series of exquisite coins bearing portraits of European rulers appeared during the latter half of the fifteenth century, and it seems likely that Henry drew inspiration from these when he decided to issue his own portrait coinage. His first shilling was known as a "testoon" (from the Italian *testone*, meaning coin with a head on it). The coin's design was probably the work of the German, Alexander of Bruchsal, but the dies may have been made by a deputy.[2]

The coin was a work of outstanding artistry and succeeded in capturing the likeness of the King to a surprising degree. This achievement is readily seen by comparing the bust on the testoon's obverse with protraits of Henry. Many English coins had borne portraits of monarchs, but few resembled their subjects. A distinctive feature of the King's bust was his arched crown, reintroduced after an absence of many centuries. The date of Henry VII's magnificent testoon, the first English shilling, is generally put at 1504, although records are hazy on this point.[3]

The new coin also revived a custom which had been dormant since the time of his namesake, Henry III – that is, indicating the monarch's position in the line of rulers bearing the same name. Although one variety of testoon identifies the King merely as HENRIC and another as HENRICUS, two others designate him as HENRIC VII and HENRIC SEPTIM. The coin's reverse bears the royal arms divided by a cross. The national coat of arms was "half French" at this time, for two of the four quarters of the shield are devoted to the fleur-de-lys. This familiar French device was to remain on British coins until the reign of George III, long after the geographical or political justification for its inclusion had disappeared.

COINER AT WORK
The technique of hammered coinage, as seen on the capital of a pillar at St. Georges de Bocherville, Normandy.

THE ESSENTIALS
At the left are the two tools required for making hammered coins: the trussel (above) and the pile (below). A blank coin ("flan") is inserted between the two and a heavy blow from the hammer produces the coin. Note the trussel's cracked edge from many blows.

A "Singularly Beautiful" Coin

Around the royal arms on the reverse of the testoon appears the legend POSUI DEUM ADIUTORE MEUM (I have made God my helper). This legend, taken from the 54th Psalm, had been used on coins of previous English monarchs and was to be retained on pieces struck by other Tudor sovereigns. Very few testoons of Henry VII survive today, although examples may be seen in the leading museums. They rarely turn up in auctions and, when they do, command very high prices. Most authorities believe that the testoons of Henry VII were never struck in quantity and that this initial English shilling was only a trial issue. Whether they were issued for general circulation or as patterns, these first shillings – or testoons – set a standard of excellence which some feel has never been equalled. "The coin from the point of view of art is singularly beautiful," one scholar has noted, "and the reign of portraiture had begun in England, the profile bust from this time forth playing an important part in the decoration of the currency."[4]

How Hammered Coins Were Struck

This first English shilling was struck by the "hammered" method. As this technique was used for striking English coins right up to the reign of Charles II, it is worthwhile examining what the operation involved.

First, it was necessary for an engraver to prepare dies for the coin's two sides – the obverse (usually bearing the royal portrait) and the reverse. As the die bearing the profile of the sovereign was the more important, it became the anvil or lower die and thus would receive only an indirect blow from the hammer.

On top of this lower die bearing the monarch's portrait the workman would place a round, blank piece of metal known as a "flan." Holding this flan in place, he (or a colleague) would gently lower the upper die until it was as nearly in line with the flan and lower die as the crude system allowed. The upper die, bearing the reverse design of the coin, would then be hit from above by a hammer. The blow would cause the flan to be stamped on its two sides simultaneously. Thus stamped, the flan became a coin.[5]

It is easy to understand how this primitive technique produced coins that were unevenly struck, had cracked edges, and contained other faults. On the other hand, when one considers the limitations of the hammered method, the craftsmanship of the early moneyers is all the more admirable.

Hentry VII's efficiency, whether expressed by his fine hammered testoon or his gift of administering public affairs, has left him with an enviable reputation among British monarchs. He managed to avoid major conflicts, banned the raising of private armies, retained his throne without great difficulty, and left the country in a sound financial condition at his death. He was possibly the wealthiest of British monarchs, for at his death his personal fortune was estimated at between £1.5 million and £5.5 millions. Using a multiple of 100 to allow for inflation over four centuries, the King's fortune could have been worth up to £550 millions today.

A Shameful Coinage

Ironically, Henry VII's thriftiness was to affect the coinage of both his son and his grandson in an adverse manner. Henry VIII conceived many grand schemes, some of them expensive to implement. Among his ambitions was that of making England's navy second to none – one that resulted in 80 vessels being added to the fleet.

Although this enterprise and others proved costly, Henry stubbornly continued to carry them out. Soon hard-pressed for funds, he found temporary relief by selling church property after the dissolution of the monasteries. But this measure did little to alleviate the grave position. Eventually he turned to the debasement of the coinage as a remedy. This step involved calling in all coins with a precious metal content, melting them down, and reissuing coins of much inferior alloys. Although England's population was small and the amount of money in circulation was minute by modern standards, this single act of debasement brought Henry's treasury over £200,000[6] – or anything up to £20 million by twentieth century reckoning.

It was not until the debasement period that Henry VIII's first shillings (they were still called testoons) were struck. So as to lead the public to think the pieces were silver, their

HENRY VIII IN OLD AGE
His shillings (testoons) were not struck until near the end of his life. The reverse depicts a crowned Tudor rose.

base metal was coated with a thin layer of silver. The high places on the coin's surface were the first to rub away, thus giving Henry a nickname among his subjects of "Old Coppernose." Poet John Heywood (1497–1580) composed a series of couplets poking fun at these debased pieces:

> Testoons be gone to Oxforde, God be their speede:
> To study in Brasen nose, there to procede,
> These testons looke redde: how like you the same?
> Tis a token of grace: they blushe for shame.

Henry VIII's Holbein-type Shilling

Except for the debased content, the testoons of Henry VIII are otherwise attractive. The King was by now plagued by bad health and his portrait on the coin is not unlike that captured by the Holbein school depicting the monarch as an aged, corpulent figure. A large Tudor rose dominates the reverse of the testoon, and is flanked by the initials H and R. Above the rose is a crown, while the circular legend, POSUI DEUM ADIUTORE MEUM, is the same as that found on Henry VII's original testoon.

The testoons of Henry VIII were struck in the Tower mint, London, and at Southwark and Bristol. The facing portrait on the obverse and the Tudor rose on the reverse are common to all three varieties, although the legends vary slightly. The Southwark piece is distinguished by the word, CIVITAS LONDON, and that of Bristol by CIVITAS BRISTOLIE.

The Clipping Curse

Although the practice of clipping the outer rims of coins probably reached its peak during the Stuart dynasty, it had already come to be recognized as a serious crime in the reign of Henry VIII. The owner of a full coin made of gold or silver, simply sheared off the circular edge and retained the clippings which he later sold for a good price. Meanwhile the coin was passed on in trade – frequently being subjected to further clipping – all the while becoming smaller. Yet the possessor always insisted on receiving full face value for the coin in the market place.

Henry VIII vowed to halt this nefarious practice, but he proved to be no more successful than monarchs before or after him. A noted chronicler of the period, Robert Fabyan, recorded that in the 37th year of Henry's reign, ". . . a woman should have been brente in Smithfielde for clipping . . . but the King's pardon came, she beying at the stake, redy to be brente."[7]

PROPAGANDA DEVICE
The Tudor rose (above) signalled the end of old rivalries and the emergence of a unified state. It appeared on many Tudor coins and was popular as an architectural design. A fine example (left) may be seen at Gloucester's City Museum.

When Henry died in 1547 at the age of 56, he left the country's finances in a chaotic condition but, to his credit, developed the British Navy into a formidable force. Despite his autocratic rule and his execution of several prominent figures (including two of his wives), Henry remained popular with his subjects.

The King Who Died a Teenager

Edward, Henry VIII's only son, came to the throne when only nine years old. Before his death at 15, he made a gallant effort to restore the coinage to the standard it was before the debasement instituted by his father.

Some scholars regard Edward as one of the most gifted of the Tudor monarchs and certainly he demonstrated remarkable abilities for one so young. He kept a diary which records most of the principal events of his brief reign. Deeply sensitive about the state of his coinage, he referred to it several times in his journal.

If the youthful King had been embarrassed by the "Old Copper Nose" testoons of his father, he must have been more humiliated when his own shillings first appeared in 25% silver and 75% base metal. When crucial issues arose Edward found himself at the mercy of his Protectors, Somerset and Northumberland. It was at the latter's behest that a large quantity of Henry VIII testoons and other coins were melted down to recover silver bullion. Edward recorded the event in his journal, justifying the action on the grounds that "the debt of the realm might be paid [and] the country defended from any sudden attempts . . . ."[8]

Bishop Latimer Ridicules Edward VI's Shilling

The young King's greatest discomfiture over his debased shillings probably came when the noted Protestant bishop, Hugh Latimer, seized on one of these coins as the theme for a sermon – delivered in Edward's presence.

BISHOP LATIMER
The bishop (above) often preached before Edward VI (right) and once dared to criticize the King's shilling in a sermon.

"We have here," preached the Bishop, "a pretty little shillyng' indeed a very pretty one. I have but one I thynke in my purse, and the last day I had put it away almost for an old grote, and so I trust some will take them. The finesse of the silver I cannot see, but therein is printed a fine sentence, that is, TIMOR DOMINI FONS VITAE & SAPIENTIAE. The feare of the Lord is the fountayne of lyfe or wisdome."[9]

Some of Edward's supporters wanted to arrest Latimer then and there for sedition, but the King would not agree. In a subsequent sermon, Latimer vigorously defended his stand, and no further effort was made to detain him.

Two superb portraits appear on Edward's shillings and contradict the impression that the king was always a sickly lad. While not so robust as his father at a similar age, Edward nonetheless enjoyed sports and made frequent mention of his athletic exploits in his diary. Many high-born youths of his own age were thrown into his company, but he had little to do with any except the lively Barnaby Fitzpatrick, the son of an obscure Irish peer. He was to write Barnaby, who went to France to complete his education, a series of extraordinary letters – some of which reflect the charm of their boyish friendship. That Edward was precocious there is little doubt; he could conjugate Latin verbs before he was eight and later mastered both Frnech and Greek. He also wrote a treatise advocating a vague kind of Common Market in which Southampton would become an international port. Fortunately, many beautiful examples of his shillings survive to bear witness to his handsomeness and lively spirit.

The First English Shilling to be Dated

Edward's first shillings depict him facing to the right and are dated 1548. This marked the first time that English coins bore dates. (There is a pattern shilling of Edward's dated a year earlier, but it was not struck in quantity.) The 1548 coin is the one referred to by Bishop Latimer in his sermon, bearing the TIMOR, etc., legend. On the reverse is the same shield found on his father's testoon, except that it is oval-shaped and ornately decorated.

THE THREE TUDOR KINGS

Henry VII (left) gave England its first shilling in the form of a testoon probably modelled after the Duke of Milan's own "head-piece," or *testone*. Henry VIII (centre) left behind a testoon bearing a likeness based on the Holbein school portraits. Edward VI (right) had an attractive shilling in fine silver, and others that were debased.

The initials E and R flank the shield. These first shillings of Edward were struck at Durham House.

The second period of Edward's coinage brought a shilling of similar design, but bearing a different legend: INIMICOS EIUS INDUAM CONFUSIONE (As for his enemies, I shall clothe them with shame: Psalm 103). Some of the second-period shillings are dated MDXLIX, others are undated. Some were struck in London, and others at Bristol and Canterbury. The base shillings of this reign are dated MDL and MDLI; these were later countermarked in Elizabeth I's reign to indicate reduced value.

It is Edward's "fine" shilling which is most commonly seen today. The "fine" refers not to the coin's appearance (although it is an extremely pleasing piece), but to the higher silver content. This shilling almost restored the coin to its former standard, and was the last to bear the name of the young monarch. His crowned bust, facing forward, is flanked on one side by the Tudor rose and on the other by the coin's value, XII. It is significant that Edward's coins continued to bear the Tudor rose, for the device was a propaganda symbol representing the Tudor concept of unity between the former Lancastrian and Yorkist factions. The reverse of Edward's last shilling carries the familiar POSUI legend encircling a plain shield on a cross.

The Shove-board and the Shilling

If Edward took some comfort towards the end of his life from partially restoring his coinage to the old standard, he would have been displeased had he been able to foresee the use of his shillings throughout the land in various "shove" games. So great was the abuse of this attractive coin that London's water-poet, John Taylor, first wrote a verse praising its beauty and, afterwards, one deploring its demise on the shove-board:

SHILLINGS OF EDWARD VI
Shown at the left is a pleasing portrait of the young King on his "fine shilling." The Tudor rose and the coin's value may also be seen on the obverse. At the right is Edward's debased shilling which was to be greatly devalued by Elizabeth I.

About my circle, I a Posie have
The title God unto the King first gave,
The circle that encompasseth my face
Declares my Soveraigne's title, by God's grace . . ..

Then Taylor went on to lament the coin's fate:

You see my face is beardless, smoothe and plaine,
Because my soveraigne was a child 'tis knowne
When as he did put on the English Crowne.
But had my stamp been bearded, as with haire,
Long before this it had beene worne and bare.
For why? With me the unthrifts every day,
With my face downwards do at shove-board play . . ..[10]

When the first Tudor king ascended the English throne, he gave England its shilling in the form of a testoon. Now, by the death of the last Tudor king, the coin had become so well established that it had become a national gaming coin.

Edward's Shove-board Shillings in Shakespeare

No less an authority than Shakespeare confirms that the shillings of Edward VI were the chosen coins for the popular shove-board (or "shovelboard") games of the time. These shillings were far more plentiful than the testoons of Henry VIII and they were infinitely more attractive. In "The Merry Wives of Windsor" Pistol, in reply to Falstaff's question, "Did you pick Master Slender's purse?" replies:

"Aye, by these gloves, did he, or I would I might never come in mine own great chamber again else, of seven groats in mill-sixpences, and two Edward shovelboards that cost me two shillings and two pence apiece of Yead Miller, by these gloves."[11]

LADY JANE GREY (RIGHT)

No shillings were struck in her name.

BEFORE EXECUTION

Lady Jane Grey faced her execution
bravely and calmly, as shown in an old
print reproduced below.

The intriguing question of how good Edward VI would have been as King had he lived to
adulthood must forever remain a matter of conjecture. While the influence of Northumberland and Somerset over him was great, nonetheless the young ruler reveals many mature
qualities in his writings. One person who knew him well was Bishop Hugh Latimer. Of
Edward's abilities he had no doubt. "I will tell you this, I will speak what I think," he said.
"His Majesty hath more godly wit and understanding, more learning and knowledge at this
[his present] age, than twenty of his progenitors that I could name had any time in their
lives."[12]

Edward's death precipitated a scheme by Northumberland to deprive Mary, the
deceased King's half-sister, of her right to the throne of England. The ambitious Northumberland had persuaded Edward to name Lady Jane Grey, wife of Northumberland's son, as
the next sovereign. Poor Jane, a talented and beautiful young woman, had no wish to

"WS" MONOGRAM
This appears on Bristol shillings struck when Sharington was under-treasurer and mintmaster.

WILLIAM SHARINGTON (RIGHT)
An opportunist, Sharington struck counterfeit shillings, then falsified the records. He was sent to the Tower of London, but escaped execution when he made a lengthy confession implicating others.

proceed with the royal charade, but had no choice. Her reign lasted only nine days. At various times claims have been put forth that coins were struck in Jane's name, but these have never been proved and it is generally agreed by scholars that no coins were issued during her brief reign.

Lacock Abbey and William Sharington

One of the oldest and most famous of English abbeys, Lacock, has an indirect association with Edward VI's Bristol shillings. The abbey, founded in 1232 and dissolved in 1539 – when its nuns were given pensions, was acquired by William Sharington, a Tudor opportunist. He retained most of the abbey's medieval features and employed the finest craftsmen of the period to carry out desired alterations and additions.

In 1546 Sharington was appointed under-treasurer, a post that gave him authority over the Bristol mint. The coins struck under his authority bear the initials, WS, and were issued in 1546 and 1547. After being in charge of the Bristol mint only three years, Sharington fell from grace when his greed and ambition led him to support Lord Seymour of Sudeley in his nefarious attempt to grab power. Seymour, brother of Edward, Lord Protector to the young King, sought to usurp his brother's authority. His ambitious schemes required money and, in his quest for it, found Sharington a useful ally. In part, Sharington's dishonesty may also have been stimulated by his need for large sums to convert Lacock Abbey into his residence.

After being indicted in early 1548, Sharington admitted to having clipped money worth £4,000 and to making counterfeit shillings (and possibly other denominations) valued at £12,000 – enormous sums for the period. He also was found guilty of falsifying his records and destroying others. His property was immediately sequestrated and he was sent to the Tower and for a time must have feared for his life, for the clipping crime alone was sufficient to merit the death penalty. For confessing his misdeeds Sharington was let off with a heavy fine. Bishop Hugh Latimer considered Sharington "an honest man," despite the lengthy

LACOCK ABBEY, POSSIBLY CONVERTED WITH SHILLINGS

One of the most popular of National Trust properties, Lacock Abbey (above) was acquired by William Sharington in the reign of Henry VIII. An unscrupulous man, Sharington became master of the mint at Bristol where he clipped coins and counterfeited shillings. His crimes may have been motivated in part by his quest for money to convert the abbey into his residence. The conversion was carried out with great care and with the help of the best artisans.

confession and added that the former Bristol mint master was "one that God loveth." Today Sharington is most remembered for preserving Lacock Abbey, one of the most popular of the National Trust properties.

III
Two Queens – and a Bard

". . . as we see on coins the different faces of persons, we see on them too their different habits and dresses, according to the mode that prevailed in the several ages . . .."

Joseph Addison.

One of England's most delightful shillings, the renowned Philip and Mary issue, appeared during a turbulent period of the Tudor dynasty.

Mary Tudor, as the elder of Henry VIII's daughters, was entitled to the throne. The public did not like the effort to install Lady Jane Grey, and news of this plot only served to increase the support for Mary. At this stage in her life, she was a symbol of the old Tudor courage and fighting spirit so characteristic of her father.

But Mary's popularity was destined to be short lived, for she wanted to make England a Catholic nation – then, and for the future. She was set on taking a Catholic as husband and producing a Catholic heir to the English throne.

An Unfortunate Marriage

By-passing all the English candidates for her hand, Mary decided to marry her cousin, Prince Philip of Spain. Philip could not have been a more ardent Catholic: his father was Emperor Charles V, ruler of the Holy Roman Empire. Immediately, Mary's popularity dropped. Discontent arose throughout the land, and violence erupted. Opposition to the proposed marriage led to military action, and a brief campaign led by Sir Thomas Wyatt almost resulted in the capture of London. Mary's followers prevailed, however, and to minimize risks, they arranged for the wedding to take place in Winchester Cathedral. There, on July 25th, 1554, Philip and Mary were wed as "equals," a herald having arrived suddenly from Italy bearing the news that Philip was now King of Naples.

Little time was wasted in producing new coinage which was to include a shilling with a most pleasing arrangement. Philip and Mary were portrayed facing each other after the style of the lovely Spanish gold escudos of Ferdinand and Isabella a half-century before. This adaptation from previous Spanish coinage suggests that Philip may have influenced the English moneyers in their choice of design.

Samuel Butler's Couplet

Philip's sharp features are emphasized by his pointed beard and coat of armour. Mary strikes a most becoming pose in her dainty bonnet. No wonder this lovely coin led Samuel Butler (1612–1680) to compose an epigram which was much quoted three centuries ago:

> Still amorous, and fond, and billing
> Like Philip and Mary on a shilling.[1]

PHILIP AND MARY
England became engulfed in religious controversy and violence after Philip (left) married Mary at Winchester in 1554. Consternation increased when Philip's foreign titles appeared on English shillings and other coins.

If the royal couple appeared happy on their shilling, the opposite was nearer the truth in real life. Philip was not happy in his uneasy role, for he had never been accepted by the English people and was not trusted by those in authority. Encountering hostility at every turn, he eventually abandoned the Queen and returned to Spain. He came back only once, and then only to enlist Mary's help against France. Although she gave it, the fighting proved disastrous for England: her old foothold in France, the port of Calais, was lost.

If the Tudor rose symbol on earlier English coins had been viewed by the public as a royal intention to maintain peace at home, the citizens of Philip and Mary's day had good cause for alarm over the legend which now appeared on coins of the reign. Reading PHILIP Z MARIA D G R ANG FR NEAP PR HISP, it stated that Philip was not only King of Naples and Prince of Spain, but also King of England. While Philip was never crowned in England, the grouping of his and Mary's titles made many people fear that England might one day become a mere province of Spain and, indeed, see the Catholic faith imposed on the entire population. thus the new coins with their ambiguous titles helped to refuel the fires of religious animosity.

These first 'full-title" shillings were dated 1554; a year later the foreign titles were

SHILLING CONTROVERSY
When the first shilling of Philip and Mary (left) appeared with the foreign titles of Philip, many people feared England's independence was at risk. The next issue (right) tactfully omitted the foreign titles, retaining only the English ones.

dropped and the legend revised to read simply REX ET REGINA ANGL. Yet the Queen's affection for Philip did not waver. "Mary's love for him," one scholar observed, "may be said to be typified by the fact that, not content with placing his name as king upon the coins, she ... joined his effigy to her own, whilst the crown, which she was unable to bequeath to him, was poised in mid-air between her consort and herself."[2]

Mary is most remembered for her persecution of Protestants. Several hundred were to lose their lives at her command – among them Bishop Latimer who had deplored the base shillings of Edward VI. Philip, by contrast, was more tolerant. He advised Mary to pardon Princess Elizabeth, not to appoint the bigoted Bishop Thirlby as Chancellor, and – in his last message to the Queen before her death – asked that she place no obstacle in the way of Elizabeth's right to succession.

Aside from the attractive facing busts and the awkward affair of Philip's foreign titles, the shillings of this reign are fascinating for their radical departure in design from previous Tudor coins. The old Tudor favourite among the religious legends had been POSUI, etc., (I have made God my helper). Mary undoubtedly wished to retain the verse, but the singular person subject was hardly appropriate for two reigning monarchs. Should she omit the legend altogether, or rewrite the Holy Word in some way? She decided on the latter course, and the legend appears in the plural form: POSUIMUS DEUM ADIUTOREM NOSTRUM (*We* have made God *our* helper), the italics being the author's.

A Shilling to Alarm the Populace

If Philip's foreign titles worried the populace, they were hardly consoled when they turned the shilling over and viewed the reverse. Here they discovered not just the familiar arms of England with the fleur-de-lys but those of the Hapsburgs as well. The new portion bore heraldic elements representing Castile and Aragon, as well as those of Austria, Naples, and Burgundy. Given position and space equal to the English half of the shield, the new device must have alarmed and bewildered the beholders.

BISHOPS LATIMER (RIGHT) AND RIDLEY AT THE STAKE
Latimer, the devout Protestant who spoke out against the debased shillings of
Edward VI, was one of many who died as Queen Mary attempted to reestablish
England as a Catholic nation. The spot where Latimer and Ridley died is marked
by a bronze cross sunk into the road in Oxford's Broad Street.

The standard of silver in coin of the realm continued to be a subject of some concern to
the public. Although the shillings and other denominations of Philip and Mary were not
debased during their reign, they did not reach the same standard found in the better coins
of Henry VII, Henry VIII and Edward VI. As will be seen, restoration to an acceptable
standard was not achieved until the following reign.

The shilling's facing-busts obverse and its shield reverse are common to all varieties of
these pieces, but the "full titles" and "English titles only," plus dates (1554, 1555, or no
dates at all), make possible an interesting assortment of specimens. There exist forgeries of
the 1554 English titles type and a non-existent 1557 variety.

That the charming Philip and Mary shilling has always had a strong public appeal is
evidenced by this excerpt from "The Alchemist" by Ben Jonson (1573–1637), involving
Face, the housekeeper, and Dapper, a lawyer's clerk:

PORTCULLIS TYPE
Elizabeth I, unhappy with debased coins of Henry VIII and Edward VI, had this variety of Edward's shilling countermarked with a portcullis and devalued to only four pence.

Face: Have you provided for her grace's servants?
Dapper: Yes, here are six score Edward shillings.
Face: Good!
Dapper: And an old Harry's sovereign.
Face: Very good!
Dapper: And three James shillings, and an Elizabeth groat. Just twenty nobles.
Face: O, you are too just. I would you had had the other noble in Maries.
Dapper: I have some Philip and Maries.
Face: Ay, those same are best of all: where are they?"[3]

Shillings with Ruffles

The humiliating loss of Calais early in 1558 was a blow to Mary's already fragile health; she lived only to November. Once more the people of England eagerly welcomed one of Henry VIII's daughters to the throne, and this time their faith was not misplaced. Elizabeth I was destined not only to live to a great age, but to inspire her country to new heights in achievement and glory.

One of her very first acts was to end the debased coinage which had plagued the nation since her father's time. The wretched shillings of Henry VIII and Edward VI were widely held by traders and by people of little means. She had the debased coins called in. Some were melted down and others were counter-marked. Two varieties of counter-marks placed on Edward VI shillings were most unusual, and today they are among the most sought after of the shilling series. One type is stamped with the mark of the portcullis, giving it a new value of four pence, and the other with a greyhound, indicating a new value of only two pence, one farthing.

This "crying down" of the value of the Edward VI shillings no doubt worked a great hardship on the populace, but the Queen was determined to proceed with the plan for conversion to a coinage of high standard. Even with the devalued shillings in circulation, the royal moneyers had some misgiving about taking in huge sums in debased metal and exchanging high quality coinage for it. There was no way of knowing how much inferior money was in circulation. How could the risk of a major fiscal fiasco be avoided?

The First Market Survey?

Out of this dilemma was born perhaps England's first market survey. In great secrecy, the Queen and Council dispatched teams of men to London market where they visited the

MARKET SURVEY

Agents of Elizabeth I toured markets, such as that shown here from a contemporary woodcut, to learn how much base coin was in circulation. This survey may have constituted Britain's first venture into market research.

butchers. There, under the pretence of having a wager as to the number of base coins in circulation, the agents persuaded the butchers to let them count the shillings in their tills of the various base types. When the results of this sampling were reported to the Council, it was decided that the planned change from base to a new, improved coinage, should go forward. The currency reform was started in 1560 and was completed in under two years. A bonus of three pence in the pound was paid to induce the public to give up inferior pieces. Despite some initial hesitance by the public, the reform was a great success. Nearly 632,000 lbs. of inferior coin was collected of which 244,000 lbs. (38%) was silver. When this silver was reissued in new coin and the cost of collecting the debased pieces, paying bonuses, coining the new pieces and other costs were deducted, the government had made a profit of £14,000. In this gigantic task the Queen was ably assisted by Richard Martin, her mint master, whom she knighted and who was twice named (1589 and 1594) Lord Mayor of London.

Elizabeth I's shillings are remarkably similar at first glance. Although her reign lasted 45 years and produced a flood of varieties, her bust always faces to the left, the old Tudor legends (POSUI, etc.) are retained, and the same reverse employed by her father, Henry VIII, and her half-brother, Edward VI, is kept. One minor, but interesting variation is that on some shillings the Queen is holding the sceptre, and on others she is not. On most coins the ruff, so characteristic of the Tudor age, is clearly portrayed.

The values of denominations were not indicated on Elizabeth's coins. Not that this mattered a great deal, for many of the Queen's subjects were unable to read. Some could determine a shilling by its size, but the royal moneyers did agree to placing the Tudor roses on alternate denominations as a means of aiding the public to know which coin was which. Thus, Elizabeth's sixpences bear the Tudor rose; the shillings do not, and so on.

None of Elizabeth's shillings have dates, thereby obliging the viewer to rely upon the

MILLED SHILLING
Elizabeth's milled coin (left) was superb, but neither the public nor mint workers welcomed it.

TO MARK CURRENCY REFORM
This medal (right) was struck to commemorate Elizabeth's currency reform of 1560.

RICHARD MARTIN
As mintmaster, he was directly responsible for Elizabeth's reform of the coinage. His wife, Dorcas, is on the reverse of the medal pictured below.

ELIZABETH'S TOMB RECORDS REFORM
The Queen was popular and her accomplishments were many; among them was the restoration of coin of the realm to its former standard. An inscription on her tomb in Westminster Abbey (above) lists this achievement.

ELIZABETH I AND HER SHILLING
The profile of the Queen on her coin above
bears a striking resemblance to her portrait at
the left.

various mint marks to determine the approximate time of issue. More than thirty mint
marks were employed on the Queen's coins, and few were retained longer than three or four
years. In some cases, mint marks have precise date relationships: the mark 0 indicates the
year 1600, the mark 1 the year 1601, and the mark 2 the year 1602. A crescent mark was
used during 1587–9, the period which embraced the defeat of the Spanish Armada. Thus,
give or take a year or two, it is possible to link Elizabeth's coins with the major historical
events of her reign.

Elizabeth's Milled Shillings

Victory over the Spanish Armada, booming trade and significant cultural achievements
were features of the Queen's long rule. Her reign also saw the beginning of milled
(machine-made) coins, although this reform did not gain permanent acceptance until the
accession of Charles II. The French had made great advances with coin-making machines,
and among their moneyers was one Eloye Mestrell who had perfected a screw-press device.
Mestrell was invited to England and soon set up his equipment. For eleven years he
produced a variety of coins, including shillings which were uniformly round and beautifully
struck. The milled shillings comprise an unusual series in that they were struck in three
sizes: small, intermediate and large.

One would think that Mestrell's future success was assured with such a brilliant achievement, but such was not the case. To begin with, the public – accustomed to hammered
coinage – viewed the nicely rounded pieces with distrust. Then, Mestrell's co-workers in the
mint – determined not to be put out of their jobs by the Frenchman's fine workmanship –
worked faster than ever, and managed to turn out hammered pieces quicker than Mestrell
could make his milled coins. With a public largely unwilling to accept machine-made coins
(for some people the opportunity to clip would be lost) and because the new process was
slower than the old one, it was inevitable that the unfortunate Mestrell should find himself
increasingly disliked.

As if he did not have problems enough, Mestrell was discovered making counterfeit coins

A COMMAND PERFORMANCE OF SHAKESPEARE
This old print shows a Shakesperian play being performed before Queen Elizabeth.
Numerous references to the shilling may be found in Shakespeare's works.

while in the employ of the mint. This offence was too much for the Queen. Pleased though she may have been with Mestrell's beautiful milled coins, she would not condone his misdeed for a moment. "Though the Queen . . . liked very well the way of making milled money . . .," one numismatist recorded, "when she knew . . . that the Monsieur who coined her money in the Mint did also at the same time counterfeit and make milled money out of the Mint, all his friends could not save him . . . [and] according to the strict laws of this nation he was condemned to death and suffered execution."[4]

As the last Tudor, Elizabeth I reached her goal of restoring English coinage to its former standard. Although this reform was resisted at first, in time it came to be regarded as one of the major accomplishments of her reign. When her tomb was erected in Westminster Abbey, part of the inscription recorded the achievement: ". . . MONETA AD IUSTUM VALOREM REDUCTA (money restored to its rightful value)."

A Shilling's Worth of Shakespeare

By the time Queen Elizabeth died in 1603, the shilling was firmly established in English literature. Shakespeare has several mentions of the coin in his plays, usually in the expected context of denoting value, for unlike the rare gold pieces held only by the wealthy, anyone knew what a shilling could buy.

He probably pays his greatest compliment to the coin in his Prologue to "Henry VIII" when he somewhat immodestly states:

> Those that come to see
> Only a show or two, and so agree
> The play may pass, if they be still and willing
> I'll undertake may see away their shilling
> Richly in two short hours.

IV
The Early Stuarts and the Amazing Civil War Coinage

"An honest shilling is better than a Knavish sovereign."

Old proverb.

With Elizabeth I's passing, the Tudor dynasty was brought to an end. England now looked to the north for its next King, James VI of Scotland, who became James I of England.

The new monarch, born in Edinburgh Castle and the son of Mary Queen of Scots, was crowned King of Scotland at the age of one and a half. With such solid Scottish connections, it was not surprising that James should wish his coins to reflect his Scottish origin. In fact, he took a keen interest in the nation's coinage and visited the mint, volunteering specific suggestions about designs and inscriptions.

As the first King to rule over both Scotland and England, James felt the heraldic device on his coins should reflect the proud heritage of both countries, so one of his first acts was to have the rampant lion and the thistle of Scotland added to the English armorial elements. Thus the redesigning of the coin of the realm was a step forward in the long development of the British nation. The formal union of Scotland and England was not, however, to be completed until the reign of the last of the Stuarts (Queen Anne).

James I's Appeal to Religion on his Shillings

Religious legends feature prominently on the coins of the early Stuarts, and for very good reasons. The Protestant–Catholic animosity that developed under the Tudors had subsequently been all too near the surface of English life. Some people were concerned lest James should institute pro-Catholic policies and once more engulf the country in religious turmoil. James himself must have understood this concern, for the legend selected for his first shillings (and other coins) expressed his hope for a tranquil reign: EXURGAT DEUS DISSIPENTUR INIMICI (Let God arise and his enemies be scattered).

Except for the variety of religious legends employed on them, the shillings of the first Stuart king are generally similar. The coins of James (except for a few gold pieces) show him facing to the right, in contrast to those of Elizabeth which portray her facing to the left. This alternating pattern has been followed in designing coin of the realm right up to the present, with two exceptions – the coins of the Civil War period and those of Edward VIII. The custom of depicting the monarch crowned continued in James' reign, and was not to be altered until Charles II's milled coinage of 1663.

The first religious legend, EXURGAT etc., used on James' shillings, was discontinued after only two years, perhaps indicating some royal apprehension that a peaceful reign would endure. In its place, on James' second shillings which appeared during 1604–19, was a new plea: QUAE DEUS CONIUNXIT NEMO SEPARET (Those whom God hath

JAMES I AND ONE OF HIS SHILLINGS
The first of England's Stuart monarchs, James (left), believed in the "divine right" of monarchs. His early shilling (above) appropriately bears a religious legend.

SCOTTISH AND IRISH DEVICES
James I was the first British monarch whose shillings (above) would display the rampant lion of Scotland and the harp of Ireland. The remainder of the royal arms (right) is shared by devices of England and France.

joined together let no man put asunder). This call for national unity is adapted from the familiar text found in the 19th Chapter of St. Matthew's Gospel.

Although there were three coinages during James I's reign, the designs of his shillings did not depart greatly from the rather austere crowned bust obverse and the heraldic shield reverse. His beard is more prominent on some varieties than others and his hair is variously trimmed, but taken as a group James I's shillings are surprisingly similar when one considers the reign lasted for more than two decades.

CROSS CALVARY

The cross calvary mintmark appears just above the crown on this hammered shilling of Charles I.

Provenance Marks to Indicate Source of Metal

So-called "provenance marks" were sometimes placed on coins to indicate the source of the bullion from which they were struck. These marks were used frequently in the Stuart and Hanoverian dynasties and, together with mintmarks denoting approximate dates, they form an interesting array of coin "clues." The first shilling to signal the origin of its metal content was one of James I bearing the well known plumes of the Prince of Wales indicating the silver mines of Wales. The plumes variety was not issued until late (1621) in James' reign and is among the rarest of the monarch's shillings.

To his credit, James I should be seen as presiding over the realm at a time when an infant "united" kingdom was emerging. At his death, he left behind shillings which, for the first time, proclaimed the monarch to rule MAGNAE BRITANNIAE (Great Britain), instead of only England as heretofore.

Charles I inherited an uneasy relationship with the English Parliament. This derived largely from James' insistence on the divine right to rule – a theory Charles was quick to endorse. Confrontation with Parliament was thus inevitable. The King was blunt in denouncing the legislative body and sometimes would call it together and then dismiss it abruptly. Eventually he decided he could get along without its members and refused to call them into session for more than ten years. This continuing controversy gradually split the people into two opposing factions – those supporting the King and those backing Parliament. In fostering this division of the population, Charles was to seal his own fate.

Charles I and "Divine Rule"

Meanwhile, his coins – not too different from those of his father except for the change in portrait – continued to be struck at the Tower mint. For any who doubted the Stuart theory of divine rule, the legend on Charles I's shillings made clear the monarch's message: CHRISTO AUSPICE REGNO (I reign under the auspices of Christ).

Silver from Welsh mines continued to be used for making some of the shillings and other coins of Charles I, and this was indicated by the plumes mintmark above the royal shield on the reverse of these pieces. Placing the actual date of issue on English coins was not yet an established custom; some monarchs had done so, but others had not. Not until the Civil Wars and the ensuing Commonwealth period was there a consistent effort to date coins. Nonetheless, the use of mintmarks had already begun when the first shilling (the testoon) was issued by Henry VII, and most such marks had a life of only a few years – thus enabling the date of issue to be reckoned fairly accurately.

THE MINTMARKS OF CHARLES I

An interesting feature of Britain's hammered coins is the number and variety of mintmarks (sometimes called "initial marks) that are shown. They help to date coins when dates are not given, and some identify mint locations and the sources of silver used in coining.

Lis (1625)		Crown (1635–6)	
Cross calvary (1625–6)		Tun (1636–8)	
Blackamoor's head (1626–7)		Anchor (1638–9) See above	
Castle (1627–8)		Triangle (1639–40)	
Anchor (1628–9)		Star (1640–1)	
Heart (1629–30)		Triangle-in-circle (1641–3)	
Plume (1630–1)		P in brackets (1643–4)	
Rose (1631–2)		R in brackets (1644–5)	
Harp (1632–3)		Eye (1645)	
Portcullis (1633–4)		Sun (1645–6)	
Bell (1634–5)		Sceptre (1646–9)	

BRIOT'S SHILLING

Another Frenchman, Nicholas Briot, designed this magnificent milled shilling of Charles I.

Mintmarks form a fascinating aspect of numismatics and scholars have devoted years of study to them. The reasons why some marks were employed are self-evident as, for example, the plumes of the Prince of Wales to denote a coin made from Welsh silver, or the lys on Henry VIII's shillings to indicate England's ancient claims on France (Calais and Dunkirk).

The coins of Charles I bear more mintmarks than those of any other English ruler. This is because his reign was somewhat long, was momentous, and saw his shillings and other coins being struck at many places outside London. Some mintmarks are royal devices (the crown and the sceptre), some have religious significance (the Cross Calvary, the Cross pattée, and the floriated cross), others speak of men at war (castle, portcullis, pellet and bugle), some reflect the garden and the forest (the rose, grapes, pear, and acorn); others represent members of the animal kingdom (lion, leopard, bird, and boar).[1]

The reign of Charles I was to be the last in which most coin of the realm was struck by the hammered method. While hammered coins by their very appearance speak of antiquity and history, they varied enormously in quality of execution because of the limitations of the method by which they were struck. The blank flans were not always round and often varied in thickness. If the moneyers did not strike their dies with solid, even blows, poor impressions resulted. Thus, Charles was far from pleased and wished for something better. His chance came when a French engraver, Nicholas Briot, emigrated to England.

Another Try at Milled Coinage

One noted numismatist, the late Sir Charles Oman, calls Briot the "Van Dyck of medallic art,"[2] and no one disputes the majestic quality of his work. Charles I, in his moment of need, learned that Briot was in London and promptly brought him into the mint, giving him wide – but not total – authority. His influence was felt immediately, despite the natural reluctance of some of his colleagues to cooperate with a foreigner. By 1631–2, the mint was using the screw press Briot had brought over, and the shillings now produced were probably the most beautiful since those of Henry VII. Moreover, they were perfectly round and evenly struck.

In 1635, Briot was sent to Edinburgh to operate the Scottish mint, and later to York, where he established a provincial mint. Later, when the Civil Wars began and the King's forces had to be paid, some of his dies were scattered right round the country in hastily established provincial mints. Briot died in 1646, the same year that his royal patron surrendered. Years later, after Charles II had come to the throne, Briot's widow filed an appeal for a pension to alleviate her penniless condition. She won her case, and lived out her life in decent circumstances.

OXFORD: CHARLES I'S "CAPITAL" FOR MORE THAN THREE YEARS
The King stayed initially at Christ Church and later Queen Henrietta Maria took
rooms at Merton. His "parliament" met in Christ Church Hall, his ammunition
was stored in New College's cloisters, and Merton's garden was the favourite
rendezvous for members of the court.

But let us return to Charles I at the time when the clouds of civil war were gathering. The
King was hard-pressed for revenue because of his determination to ignore Parliament, the
body normally charged with fund-raising. In desperation, he resorted to unusual and
unpopular measures, such as "ship money," revived from medieval times. Formerly, taxes

had been levied on coastal towns to help finance the Navy. Charles now required inland towns and counties to contribute funds for the Navy. He also sold monopoly rights to favoured merchants. These and other measures exacerbated the painful division of the country. By now it was clear that conflict was inevitable; the only question was how soon it would erupt.

Charles' long-running feud with Parliament came to a head in 1642 when he attempted to arrest several members of Parliament. This effort was taken by Parliament as an unforgivable affront to its authority, and soon the nation was plunged into civil war.

The Nation's Coinage in Disarray

Coinage was at once affected by the dramatic turn in events. The King fled to the provinces, taking up residence at Oxford and other places that afforded refuge. Parliament, meanwhile, continued to issue coinage in the name of Charles at the Tower mint.

Unlike conventional wars in which armies occupy specific battle lines, the Civil Wars were a series of actions – often unrelated – involving relatively small forces. However isolated the Royalist forces were, they had to be paid, and their supplies had to be purchased from such local sources as were available. The only course open to the King was that of establishing mints in those regions of England and Wales where his forces held sway.

Oxford, more than any other city, became the symbol of the Royalist cause. Charles was able to maintain residence here at first, although – when matters were going badly for his forces – he had to take refuge in other places. A mint was set up in New Inn Hall where a wide range of Oxford Civil War provincial coins was struck. Other places where pieces were issued, or *may* have been issued, include: Appledore, Barnstaple, Bideford, Bristol, Chester, Coombe Martin, Corfe Castle, Coventry, Exeter, Lundy Island, Salisbury, Sandsfoot Castle, Shrewsbury, Truro, Weymouth, Worcester and York. Not all these mints are confirmed, for the King's moneyers – on hearing the enemy was approaching – quickly packed up their improvised coining gear and fled to other places of safety.

Shillings have been positively identified from these Civil War provincial mints: Bristol, Coombe Martin, Exeter, Shrewsbury, Truro and York. Either Weymouth or Sandsfoot Castle also issued the shilling (and lesser coins), but it is impossible to make positive attributions. The same is true of another set, ranging from the halfcrown to the halfgroat, which could have been struck on Lundy Island or Appledore, Barnstaple and Bideford. Until and unless further documentation is found, the provenance of these Civil War pieces must remain obscure.

Although most provincial coins understandably suffered a loss of quality due to the unusual circumstances under which they were struck, those made by Briot (or from his dies), were generally of a high standard. With one notable exception, the provincial shillings offered little variation from the bust-and-shield types which marked the first period of Charles' reign. The exception was the so-called "Declaration" coin, a type whose reverse bore the inscription RELIGIO PROTESTANTIUM, LEGES ANGLIAE, LIBERTAS PARLIAMENTI (The Protestant religion, the laws of England, the liberty of Parliament). the motto is taken from the King's famous Declaration of Wellington, and first appeared on his coins issued at Shrewsbury. Although Charles' enemies viewed the motto with contempt, the King's followers no doubt considered it an effective propaganda device, for the declaration was subsequently included on Charles' shilling at four other mints.

Mintmarks on the provincial coins are useful in identifying mints where the pieces were

"DECLARATION" TYPE
This shilling bears the famous declaration of Charles originally made at Wellington.

struck. Aberystwyth shillings usually feature an open book, those of Oxford and Bristol a plume, those of Exeter a rose. Some towns had abbreviations of their mints: OX for Oxford, BR for Bristol, and EBOR (from the Latin, EBORACUM), York.

A Dearth of Silver

As the Royalist lost to the forces of Parliament in battle after battle, the number of troops under Charles' banner was reduced and they were left in pockets without hope. Nonetheless, some continued to hold out, perpetuating the problem of finding enough money for pay and provisions.

Operating mints under field conditions was a difficult enough process for the Royal moneyers who must have uttered many times something like "Have mint – will flee," but obtaining silver for coins was at times a struggle quite apart from the fighting. At the outset of the conflict both Royalists and Parliamentarians made public appeals for donations of silver plate. The response was varied: instantaneous and generous, as well as begrudging and mean.

Londoners queued up for days to part with their cherished plate at Guildhall to show their loyalty to Parliament. In the provinces, Charles met with equal fervour. With Oxford as the unofficial capital for a while, it was perhaps inevitable that the University should see almost the whole of its ancient plate lost to the Royalist cause. To stimulate public donations, the King offered an eight per cent return (a good rate for those days) on the value of silver "loaned." The rush by citizens of both sides, perhaps motivated in some cases by hope of high office or other reward, was a favourite subject for satire. Typical of this literature are the lines of the poet, M. L. Llewellin (1616–82), who wrote:

> And now my Lord, since you have London left
>   Where Merchants' wives dine cheap, and as cheap sup,
> Where fooles themselves have of their Plate bereft,
>   And sigh and drinke in the course Pewter cuppe.
> Where's not a Silver Spoone left, not that given than,
>   When the first Cockney was made Christian.
> No, not a bodkin, pincase, all they send
>   Or carry all, whatever they can happe on,
> E'en to the pretty Picktooth, whose each end
>   Purg'd the relickes of continuall Capon.
> Nothing must stay behind, nothing must tarry.
>   No not the ring by wch. deare Joan took Harry.[3]

How People Were Parted from Their Plate

Never before and never since the English Civil War were so many citizens and institutions parted from their silver and, in some instances, gold plate. The main centres of collection remained London's Guildhall for the Parliamentarians and Oxford for Charles I's Royalist followers. Pressure had to be exerted on some reluctant donors, but in general, most citizens willingly gave up their precious possessions in the hope of seeing their favoured cause emerge victorious. A commentator, observing the success of the London plate collection, noted that "the Parliament were at that time glad to see any men's willingness and forwardnesse unto their service; they promised largely, and made some pleasing votes, so that the Plate and Moneys of the Citizens came tumbling into Guildhall upon the publique faith."[4]

Samuel Butler, in his *Hudibras*, satirized the rush of Londoners to give up their cherished plate – whether large or small items:

> Did Saints, for this, bring in their Plate,
> And crowd as if they came too late.
> For when they thought the Cause had need on't,
> Happy was he that could be rid on't.
> Did they coin Piss-Pots, Bowls, and Flaggons,
> Int' officers of horse and dragoons;
> And into pikes and musquetteers,
> Stamp beakers, cups, and porringers?
> A thimble, bodkin, and a spoon,
> Did start up living men, as soon
> As in the furnace they were thrown,
> Just like the dragon's teeth being sown.
> Then was the Cause of Gold and Plate,
> The brethen's offerings, consecrate,
> Like th' Hebrew Calf, and down before it
> The Saints fell prostrate, to adore it,
> So say the wicked.[5]

Indeed, the Parliamentry forces came to be known as the "Thimble and Bodkin Army" by the followers of the King.[6]

Oxford Colleges Made to "Lend" Their Plate

In January, 1642, Charles notified all the Oxford colleges that he was establishing a mint in the city, and expected the several colleges to cooperate in supplying it with their plate. "We are soe well satisfied with your readinesse and affection to Our Service," he said, "that We cannot doubt but you will take all occasions to express the same." Then he came to the point' "We have removed Our Mint hither to Our Citie of Oxford for the coyning thereof, And We doe hereby desire you, that you will lend unto Us all such Plate of what kind soever wch belongs to youre Colledge, Promising you to see the same justly repayde unto you after the rate of 5s. the ounce for white, and 5s. 6d. for guilt Plate as soone as God shall enable Us."[7]

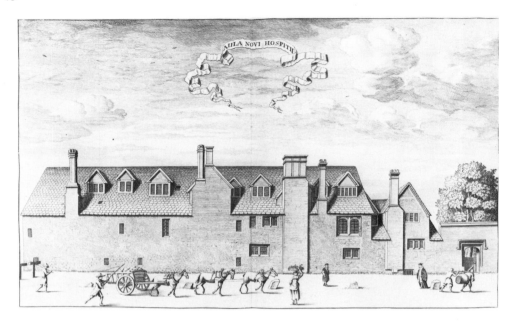

AULA NOVI HOSPITII

THE ROYAL MINT IS TRANSFERRED TO OXFORD'S NEW INN HALL
Here Charles I established his mint and it was at this building that plate belonging to the Oxford colleges was melted down and turned into coin for the Royalist cause. Because of the sacrifice of plate to support the King, very little remains from the Elizabethan and Jacobean periods at the colleges.

Much of the plate held by Oxford's colleges had been bequeathed in perpetuity and at least one college, Exeter, took up this point with the King, pointing out "that it was contrary to the statutes they were sworn to observe, to alienate or so much as alter the form of their plate, upon any pretence whatsoever."[8] But Charles was not to be denied, for he knew if he made an exception in the case of Exeter College, other colleges would immediately make the same claim. So, in his reply, the King urged Exeter to follow "the example of other colleges, who were equally tyed down in that respect by their statutes;" Charles went on to say that if Exeter only "considered the intention of their benefactors, they would make no scruple."[9] The college thereupon dropped its objection and handed over silver plate valued at £208 and gilt worth £38 for which a royal receipt was issued on February 2nd, 1642.

Correspondence and records pertaining to the passing over of plate indicate that Charles preferred the transactions to be regarded as gifts. Yet his initial letter of request allowed for the same value to be attached to the weight of all plate (five shillings per ounce for silver and 5s. 6d. for gilt), regardless of antiquity or design. It thus was not surprising that a few colleges managed to conceal a few pieces of their most beautiful or revered plate. Nonetheless, records show that 18 Oxford colleges contributed plate valued at enormous sums for those days.[10]

CARLISLE SHILLING (LEFT)
Dated 1645, this is one of two varieties of siege shillings struck at Carlisle.

NEWARK SIEGE PIECE (RIGHT)
Diamond-shaped shillings were struck at Newark in 1645 and 1646. There were also halfcrowns and pieces of ninepence and sixpence.

Four Siege Shillings

From 1644 to 1649 coins of several denominations were struck by the besieged Royalist garrisons at Carlisle, Newark, Pontefract and Scarborough. As had been the case with supporters of the opposing sides in London and Oxford, the inhabitants in the garrison towns, too, were called upon to deliver up their plate. In each of the four besieged places that issued coins the plate was sought to pay the wages of the Royalist soldiers and to provide provisions for them and their horses.

That Charles remained hopeful of retaining his crown is indicated by his order that receipts be given to all citizens who handed over plate. In Carlisle rich and poor alike backed the King's cause, as excerpts from a list made at the time reveal:

"Widdow Craister one beare boule one beaker one wine boule and six spoones wt 012-½-oz.

Edward Dalton one boule one Tumbler & 2 peeces of broken plate wt 022-0-1/8 oz.

Sr Thomas Glemham 2 Candlesticks wt 044-¾-0 oz."

Nor was the Carlisle Corporation's silver plate immune from the royal pressure, as this next item shows:

"The Citties' plate 2 Flaggons 2 gilt bowles one gilt salt 2 beare bowles wt 233-0-0 oz."[11]

The besieged towns struck a surprising number of denominations, given the difficulties under which the moneyers worked. The Carlisle garrison produced shilling and three shilling values; at Newark there were four denominations: sixpence, ninepence, shilling and halfcrown; Pontefract had a shilling and a two shilling piece in silver, and a gold unite; Scarborough, however, topped the list of denominations issued by turning out no less than 22 values ranging from a sixpence to a piece stamped five shillings and eightpence.

Although besieged, Carlisle was never attacked. Its surrender was brought about by a

SCARBOROUGH SHILLING

All the Scarborough siege pieces
were irregularly shaped.

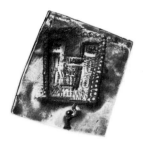

blockade which produced the desired result – a threat of starvation. The town's garrison
realized its hopeless position after the Royalist defeat at the Battle of Naseby on June 14th,
1645, and capitulated eleven days later. Contemporary records indicate that the issue of
Carlisle's siege pieces probably was undertaken by the town corporation itself. This seems
likely, given the meticulous identification and precise weights shown in the list above – the
compilation of which no doubt was the task of some conscientious civil servant. One local
chronicler affirms that the plate donations in Carlisle were made "chearfully"[12] after the
orders had been published, but had the citizens any real alternative?

The Carlisle shilling siege piece is found either in round or octagonal shape. Its obverse
bears the initials CR topped with a large crown. Beneath the monogram is the coin's
denomination, XII. The reverse is just as austere, containing only OBS CARL and the
date, 1645. One variety has the legend on the reverse in two lines, another in three.

Newark's siege pieces were struck in greater quantity than any other of the Civil War
coins of necessity and thus are the most common today. The Newark garrison fell to the
Scottish army on May 6, 1646, by the order of Charles. The surrender of the castle was a
great blow to the Royalist cause for it had successfully withstood a number of previous
sieges. All the Newark siege pieces are diamond shaped, and the designs are similar. The
obverse of the shilling bears a crown (two varieties) flanked by the initials C and R, below
which appears the value, XII. the reverse contains the simple legend, OBS NEWARK (or
NEWARKE), beneath which is the date, 1645 or 1646.

Scarborough Castle: Frantically Sheared Shillings

Scarborough Castle, which produced the most amazing array of siege pieces, fell on 22 July,
1645, after holding out for nearly a year. If other siege coins had been unusual in shape and
design, Scarborough's were destined to become more nondescript still. Here the King's
moneyers made no effort to limit their coins to a few standard denominations. Instead they
hastily sheared whatever plate they could get their hands on – bowls, trenchers, salvers, and
anything else, no matter how small. They concentrated on cutting up the plate into fragments that were approximately the size of coins of the realm, without wasting any time on
making them of uniform size or weight. Only then did they weigh each fragment and, once
the weight had been translated into the intrinsic value of silver, the coin's value was
stamped on it along with a crude representation of Scarborough Castle.

Thus it was purely by accident that the usual denominations such as shillings and halfcrowns were struck, but what unusual denominations otherwise! There was a piece of five
shillings and eightpence, one of three shillings and fourpence, another of two shillings and
tenpence – and so on. These strange values deriving from the hasty workmanship of Scar-

TWO OLD PRINTS DEPICT THE LAST HOURS OF CHARLES I

The tumultuous reign of Charles I, accompanied by the irregular coinage of the Civil War, drew to an end in January of 1649. The print at the left shows the monarch taking leave of his family, while the other portrays him at the execution block.

borough's moneyers suggest the same kind of frustration experienced by the young man on his first day of work at the grocer's while trying to cut precisely a pound of cheese. Some of the Scarborough siege pieces are unique, and all are rare.

Sir Hugh Cholmondeley was the Royalist Governor of Scarborough town and castle at the time of the siege by Parliamentary troops. He compiled a brilliant picture of the events before and during the attack, including references to the siege coins issued. Handicapped as he was in obtaining bullion or plate, Sir Hugh states that the greater part of the minting operation was borne "upon his owne chardge and purse."[13]

The Governor, with his own plate apparently used up, appealed to others in the garrison to part with theirs. This move proved unpopular. The last thing Sir Hugh wanted at this critical stage was a mutiny on his hands, so he decided to approach only those people in the garrison whom he "had perticuler interest in"[14] – a phrase obviously embracing friends and those who were under some sort of obligation to the Governor.

Sir Hugh goes on to describe what he did next:

". . . [I] . . . made use of the plaite . . . which was cutt in peeces and passed currant according to there severall weights, some of them had the stampe of a broaken Castle with this inscription 'Caroli fortuna resurgam;' by this meanes the officers and soildiors, which beganne to be verie clamourous, were for the present verie well settled . . . ."[15]

CHARLES I: A VAIN HOPE
Charles I (right) in a formal pose. His Pontefract shilling (above), struck the year before his execution, stated: "While I breathe I hope."

The Shilling that Expressed Hope

Pontefract's shillings are perhaps the most fascinating of the siege pieces. In shape, they are to be found in round, diamond or octagonal forms. On the obverse is the familiar large crown with the initials CR below. But now appears a pathetic hope in the legend, one which bespoke the desperation of the hour: DUM SPIRO SPERO (While I breathe I hope). The reverse has a representation of a castle flanked by the initials P and C (for Pontefract Castle), the OBS designation for the town's besieged status, and the date, 1648.

With such an interesting coin to its credit – for the Pontefract siege pieces had more detail in their designs than any other – the King's moneyers may have been expected to retire gracefully when Charles was executed in 1649. But this was not to be, for the final phase of the Civil Wars was still ahead. In defiance of the winning Parliamentary forces, Pontefract issued gold unites and shillings *after* the death of Charles I. The shillings, although dated 1648 and bearing obverse and reverse designs similar to the first Pontefract pieces, now have remarkable legends. Bearing the name of Charles II (CAROLUS SECUNDUS), they boldly announce how the crown was passed to the new King: HANC DEUS DEDIT (God has given this). The other legend is also a commentary on the succession: POST MORTEM PATRIS PRO FILIO (For the son after the death of the father). Charles II was not to assume the throne until the Restoration in 1660, but the daring Pontefract moneyers managed to issue coins bearing the name of the new monarch a decade before he returned to Britain.

V

The Monarchy Lost – and Restored

"When I came into the world, I found that I had been happier in my retirement than I had thought, having probably by that means escaped wearing a monstrous pair of trousers."

From Joseph Addison's "shilling tale," *The Tatler* (No. 249).

The "monstrous pair of trousers" referred to in the extract above is the unusual double-shield design on the reverse of Oliver Cromwell's Commonwealth shilling, adapted from the official arms. If Cromwell and his men had toppled the monarchy, they were no less successful in bringing about a startling change in the appearance of the country's coinage.

Religious controversy motivated many who fought in the Civil Wars and it was a Cromwellian reaction to the Stuart dynasty's belief in rule by divine right that probably led to the emission of Latin from the Commonwealth coins. Catholic influence had grown at the Court of Charles I, and Cromwell's followers may have thought that Latin inscriptions were inappropriate for coins of the Commonwealth. Thus the new coins, including the shilling, bore wording only in English and the general appearance of the Commonwealth series is one of utmost austerity. One may surmise that Cromwell wished for no trace of ostentation on his coinage. Instead the obverse bears a simple shield containing the Cross of St. George, surrounded by the legend: THE COMMONWEALTH OF ENGLAND. It is interesting to note, whether by design or otherwise, that the realm is no longer called "Great Britain," as it was in the reigns of James I and Charles I.

The "Breeches" Shilling of the Commonwealth

The reverse of the Commonwealth shilling (and all of the coins in this series were of similar design) bears the double-shield device previously mentioned. One comprises St. George's cross, the other the harp of Ireland; it was the joining together of the two shields which made the device look like a pair of breeches and thereby gave the monarchists a satirical talking point. The breeches, they said, were a "fit stamp" for the "Rump" – a reference to the so-called "Rump Parliament" of Cromwell which was composed almost entirely of his own followers after those loyal to Charles had either fled or been expelled. The only inscription on the shilling is the date, value (XII), and a circular legend reading GOD WITH US. Not content with their breeches reference, the monarchists also pointed out that, on Cromwell's coins, God was on one side and the Commonwealth on the other. There are shillings dated for each year of the Commonwealth era (1649–60) except 1650.

Although rejecting the title of King, Cromwell eventually agreed to an issue of coins bearing his portrait. Numismatists are divided as to whether this second issue of the Commonwealth period was a legitimate issue, or merely patterns. Certainly the number struck was not great, for all are rare. Yet some – especially shillings and halfcrowns – turn up in used condition. The first of these coins was struck before Cromwell's death, but it seems they may not have circulated immediately. This mystery ever their true status is not helped when one examines the order, issued early in the reign of the restored Charles II, calling in

NO PORTRAIT
The Commonwealth shilling is the only one in the denominational series of coin of the realm without a portrait.

CROMWELL SHILLING
Although Oliver Cromwell (left), refused to accept the title of King, he nonetheless allowed a crown to be placed on the reverse of his shilling (above) and other coins.

all coins of "the late usurpation" bearing the words "THE COMMONWEALTH OF ENGLAND." Why, if Charles II wished to remove from circulation *all* coins of the Commonwealth period, did he not include the pieces bearing Cromwell's bust?

Perhaps all the facts surrounding the issue of the Cromwell shillings and other denominations will never be known; what is clear, however, is that these pieces rank among the most beautiful coins ever struck in Britain. The designs were executed by Thomas Simon who had been named by Cromwell as graver to the mint in the same year (1656) they were first dated.[1] At last, here was an Englishman whose workmanship compared favourably with that of the foreigners. In an inferior position, Simon had dutifully worked on the simplistic Commonwealth coins. It is easy to imagine that his patience may have been severely tried in turning out coins with such unimaginative designs.

Cromwell's Emperor-Type Shilling

Now, as graver and charged with the task of producing a new set bearing the Lord Protector's bust, Simon had a free hand and his enthusiasm and diligence is borne out by the exquisite workmanship found on the new pieces. There is no suggestion of a royal personage in the coin's legend, but Cromwell's powerful bust is another matter. Here, is the unmistakable laureated bust so reminiscent of Roman emperors. A strange contradiction

CROMWELL EXPELLING PARLIAMENT
This contemporary Dutch satirical print shows members of Parliament being expelled in 1653. Above Cromwell's head in the rear of the House may be seen the arms of the Commonwealth that featured so prominently on coins of the era.

appears when one turns over Cromwell's shilling and studies the reverse: anti-monarchist that he was, Cromwell allowed a crown to be positioned above his shield.

The Cromwell pieces are interesting for other reasons as well. Whereas the formerly despised Latin was omitted from the regular Commonwealth coins, it returns to favour on Cromwell's own money. One theory is that the poet, John Milton, who was Cromwell's Latin secretary, brought his influence to bear when the coin designs were being approved. Whatever the explanation, there is not a word of English on Cromwell's pieces – a total reversal of the situation that existed on his earlier, Commonwealth coins.

Unlike the regular Commonwealth coins which stated only THE COMMONWEALTH OF ENGLAND, Cromwell's own pieces revert to the former custom of listing the several areas of Great Britain. Circling the laureated bust of Oliver Cromwell is a Latin legend proclaiming him Protector of ANG SCO ET HIB (England, Scotland, and Ireland).

The Peace-through-War Shilling

The reverse of Cromwell's shilling (and other denominations) contains a heraldic device which is unique on British coins. The anachronistic crown already has been cited, but the

THE KING RETURNS
This Dutch print of 1661 depicts the entry of Charles II into London, an event also recorded by John Evelyn, the diarist. The King's return also was to mean the end of hammered coins for Britain.

shield beneath it is also unusual. Divided into four quarters, it accords one to Scotland by embràcing the Cross of St. Andrew, and one to Ireland by reproducing the familiar harp. The other two quarters show a favourite Cromwell symbol – the Cross of St. George. But the stamp of the Lord Protector does not end here; in the centre of the shield is superimposed Cromwell's lion rampant. Moreover, there is a legend in Latin stating the Cromwellian justification for the regime's military emphasis: PAX QUAERITUR BELLO (Peace is sought by war).

After the death of his father, Richard Cromwell attempted to take his place as leader. In this effort he failed miserably and it soon became clear that Charles Stuart should be invited back to Britain. There was no distinctive coinage issued in the name of Richard Cromwell, although the last of the Commonwealth series – those bearing the anchor initial mark – appeared both before Oliver's death and during Richard's time as Lord Protector.

The Commonwealth coins were hammered, but before the era was over, the old battle between supporters of hammered coins and milled ones was resumed in the mint. Peter Blondeau, an experienced Paris engraver, came to England in 1649 at the invitation of Cromwell's Council. He brought with him an improved version of the French milling machine. Immediately the old feuds erupted, and the uneasy Frenchman was set upon on all sides – including attacks by public pamphlets. It was the same old story of resistance to change; the old employees maintained they could produce better coins, and at a faster rate, than could Blondeau with his modern equipment. A contest proved inconclusive, but at least Blondeau was not dismissed.

By the time approval had been received for the set of coins bearing Cromwell's effigy, Blondeau teamed with Thomas Simon to produce the splendid set already described. But by now the Protectorate was falling into disarray and only a small quantity of the Cromwell coins were struck. Blondeau, sensing his period of usefulness was over, returned to France

CHARLES II: OLD TYPE COIN
Returning to Britain after exile abroad, Charles II (right) had to wait several years before his milled coinage could be initiated. His last hammered shilling is pictured above.

while he could. Following his departure, mint officials lost no time in packing up the Frenchman's equipment and shipping it to Edinburgh. It was through this act that the Edinburgh mint was later able to turn out coins of outstanding beauty and which, at the time they appeared, were superior to anything being produced in London.

Charles II did not come by the crown easily. As a young man he had been with his father at the Battle of Edgehill, then – after the Royalist defeats in 1646 – had fled to the Scilly Isles and thence to France. Just after his twentieth birthday, he landed in Scotland and six months later was crowned as King of the Scots at Scone. But his effort to win over Cromwell ended with defeat at Worcester in September of 1651, after which he once more had to flee to France.

The Return of Charles II

During the Commonwealth era Charles wandered about Europe, impatient for the moment when he could return and take up his father's mantle. After Richard Cromwell showed himself incapable of ruling, Charles was asked to return to Britain. His triumphant entry into London on May 29, 1660, was witnessed by the diarist John Evelyn:

> The Mayor, aldermen, all the companies in their liveries, chains of gold, banners; lords and nobles, cloth of silver, gold and velvet everybody clad in, the windows and balconies all set with ladies, trumpets, music and myriads of people flocking in the streets, and was as far as Rochester, so as they were seven hours in passing the city, even from two in the afternoon till nine at night.[2]

For the first two years of his reign Charles II was obliged to continue the system of hammered coins which his father had hoped to end with the help of Nicholas Briot. These hammered pieces, the last such in the coinage of Britain, differed little from those of the other

Stuart monarchs except for the change in royal profile. Oddly, Charles did not follow the pattern of alternating the direction in which English monarchs had faced; instead, he elected to have his profile face to the left, as both his father (Charles I) and Oliver Cromwell had done on their coins. The shillings, and other denominations, again reminded citizens that the realm was British – not merely English – and also embraced Ireland and France: the legend read, CAROLUS II D G MAG BRIT FRAN ET HIB REX. The inclusion of France was based on Britain's claim to Dunkirk, a claim that was to be abandoned early in the reign of Charles.

The task of designing the last hammered coins of Britain was given to Thomas Simon. So anxious was the King to remove the Commonwealth coins from circulation and replace them with his own that he told Simon to commence work, "using all speed."[3] By early 1661 hammered shillings and other coins were being struck in quantity and the time was near when the despised coins of the Commonwealth could be recalled. In the month of September, Charles issued a royal proclamation, announcing that the coinage "struck during the late usurpation" and bearing the words "THE COMMONWEALTH OF ENGLAND," would be outlawed beginning December 1st.[4] An extension of several months was later granted, by which time the public could exchange the old coinage for new.

Charles II was far from happy about the state of affairs which existed at the Mint. Foremost, probably, was his displeasure at the poorly produced hammered coinage. He ordered many changes to be made and by the end of his second year as King, new policies were in operation. An end was quickly put to the small army of parasitical citizens who had virtually taken over many of the premises adjacent to the mint. Tighter security was effected, a measure which authorized personal searches of employees and others entering and leaving the mint. It also sought to halt the flow of coin dies to persons outside the mint. But the King's new broom did not end its sweep here; in mid-1661 he announced that milled coinage would be instituted as soon as possible to stop the clipping (and sometimes counterfeiting) which had plagued British monarchs for more than a century.

The "Battle" of the Engravers

Peter Blondeau was brought back from France, and from Flanders came an entire family, the Roettiers, possessed of remarkable engraving talent. Thomas Simon, like so many of his countrymen before him, had difficulty in working with the foreigners. Although Simon's ability was of the first order, the King preferred the workmanship of the Roettiers – perhaps because the senior Roettier had once befriended Charles while he was in exile. Moreover, the King likely had not forgotten that Simon had been a prominent servant of the Commonwealth.

Simon was bitterly affronted by the royal choice of Roettier and prepared a superb crown piece as a measure of his discontent at Charles' decision. This crown, called Simon's "petition piece," is considered by some as the most beautiful silver coin ever struck in Britain. Apart from its exquisite obverse and reverse, the coin bore a lengthy and passionate plea to Charles II around its rim:

> Thomas Simon most humbly prays your Majesty to compare this his tryall piece with the Dutch and if more truly drawn & emboss'd more gracefully order'd and more accurately engraven to releive him.[5]

But Simon's plea went unanswered, and Roettier's design was selected for use on the new

MILLED COINAGE AT LAST

Charles I introduced milled coinage in the 1660s and, unlike previous attempts, this one succeeded. This shilling is dated 1666, year of London's Great Fire.

milled coins. The Simon–Roettier competition must have been a popular topic of conversation, for it turns up in the diary of Samuel Pepys on March 9th, 1663, by which date the shilling and the complete range of milled pieces had been struck. Of his impression on this occasion the noted diarist writes:

> There dined with us today Mr. Slingsby of the Mint, who showed us all the new pieces, both gold and silver, examples of them all, that were made for the King by Blondeau's way; and compared them with those made for Oliver. The pictures of the latter made by Symons, and of the King by one Rotyr, a German, I think, that dined with us also. He extols those of Rotyr above the others; and, indeed, I think they are the better, because the sweeter of the two; but, upon my word, those of the Protector are more like in my mind than the King's, but both very well worth seeing.

Pepys also provides an interesting commentary on the new security arrangements brought into force at the mint in an attempt to stop the pilfering of precious metal by labourers. On May 19th, 1663, he was told about an ingenious cheat possessing rare intestinal fortitude, who conveyed away "bits of silver cut out for pence by swallowing them, and so they could not find him out, though, of course, they searched all the labourers; but, having reason to doubt him, they did, by threats and promises, get him to confess, and did find £7 of it in his house at one time."

The advent of all-milled coinage for Britain under Charles II resulted in two significant changes in the designs of coins. As if turning his back forever on the old hammered issues, Charles now reversed the direction in which his profile faced. This right-facing bust, instituted on milled coins dated 1662, was followed by coins with the left-facing profile of James II, and so on – alternating with each new monarch – until Edward VIII ascended the throne when his pattern coins broke the tradition.

The Shillings are Dated Again

The milled coinage also marked the disappearance of crowned monarchs on British shillings, with the single exception of Queen Victoria's shillings from 1887 onwards. Otherwise, the first milled shilling of Charles II has a more pleasing and less crowded design than most of the hammered series. Around the King's profile appears CAROLUS. II.DEI. GRATIA. While the reverse has a cruciform shield with a monogram of interlocking Cs in each of the four spaces of the cross. On the shield are heraldic devices representing England, Scotland, Ireland and France, and encircling it the royal title: MAG. BR. FRA. ET. HIB. REX, with the date. Although the reign of Edward VI had produced a dated shilling – the nation's first dated coin – successive monarchs did not follow a rigid policy of

SHORT-LIVED SHILLINGS
The short reign of James II permitted shillings to be struck for only four years,
1685–8.

dating all coins. Again, the new milled series incorporated the date as an essential element
of a coin's design, a feature that would hereafter be retained.

There was little change in the designs of Charles II's shillings during the remainder of his
reign with one major exception – the reintroduction of provenance marks on some coins to
denote the source of the metal used in them. The plumes of the Prince of Wales already had
been used on shillings of James I and Charles I to indicate the Welsh origin of the coins'
silver content. This Welsh marking was continued on some shillings of Charles II, and two
new ones were added – the elephant, and the elephant and castle – denoting silver supplied
by The Africa Company whose badge was the familiar elephant and castle whose memory
survives today in the name of the Elephant Tavern and the Elephant and Castle
Underground station.

Charles II died from a stroke in 1685 and the crown passed to his brother, James. To
Charles is due credit for putting Britain's coinage on a respectable basis. The repeated
attempts to adopt milled coinage, first undertaken in the reign of Elizabeth I and continued
intermittently for nearly a century, at last had succeeded.

A Short, Unhappy Reign

Few British sovereigns have known such a brief and turbulent reign as that experienced by
James II. The religious issues which divided the nation in the time of his father, Charles I,
were still being debated throughout the land. By coincidence, events in France were hardly
reassuring to the people of England who feared violence to be an inevitable consequence of
the religious confrontation between Protestants and Catholics. In particular, it was the
revocation of the Edict of Nantes (a civil rights charter for Huguenots) and the subsequent
persecution of French Protestants, that caused many Englishmen to assume that similar
oppression could occur in England under James II.

However, there is no legend or other wording on the coins of James to indicate he wished
to pursue a fervent religious campaign or any other cause. His shillings bear a simple regal
profile on the obverse with a legend, IACOBUS II DEI GRATIA, while the reverse has the
date of issue and the King's title: REX MAG. BR. FRA. ET HIB. James' shillings were
struck for only four years, 1685–8, and all are scarce or rare. They were engraved by
Roettier.

James II had not forgotten that his father, Charles I, had been executed and this
knowledge contributed to his growing distrust and fear of the English people. Concerned
about his ability to remain in control of the monarchy, he expanded the Army. His fears for
the future proved to be well founded when the Duke of Monmouth, illegitimate son of
Charles II, landed in Dorset and was hastily proclaimed "King" by his supporters. James
felt he had to deal ruthlessly with the Duke and his friends when their attempted coup
failed. Accordingly the Duke and many of his supporters were executed, others were

JAMES II: THE FLIGHT

After mass desertions to William of Orange, James II (above) realized his reign was at an end. His flight from London is pictured in the print at the right. Later, his gun-money shillings appeared in Ireland.

thrown into prison, and still others were transported abroad to penal colonies — all victims of Judge George Jeffreys and his infamous "Bloody Assizes."

Meanwhile, another figure, William of Orange — the husband of James' daughter, Mary, and a staunch Dutch Protestant — was preparing to come to England to lead a "glorious revolution." Within two months of landing at Torbay in early November, 1688, William had routed the King's forces and James was obliged to flee to France. At no time did his troops present a united front against William; James was dismayed to see some of his trusted leaders, including the highly competent John Churchill (the future Duke of Marlborough) desert to William.

But James was not to give up his crown without a fight. Back in France, he mobilized support with which he hoped to engage English forces in Ireland and from there go on to victory. (His hard-pressed campaign caused him to strike the now well-known "Irish Gun-money," an account of which is given in the chapter on Irish and Scottish shillings.)

William III defeated James at the Battle of the Boyne in July, 1690. Once more James made his way to France, this time never to return. When he died in 1701, he was buried at St. Germain-en-Laye near Paris.

VI
Clipping and William III's Recoinage

"I told you that my grandfather was a shorter," said the jockey, "by which is meant a gentleman who shortens or reduces the current coin of the realm, for which practice he was scragg'd, that is, hung by the scrag of his neck. My father reduced or shortened the coin of this country by three processes. By acqua fortis, *by clipping and by filing. Filing and clipping he employed in reducing all kinds of coins, whether gold or silver . . . From a five shilling piece . . . he would file or clip to the value of five pence, and from lesser coin in proportion."*

From *Romany Rye* by George Borrow.

By the mid-1660s milled coins were at last being produced in sufficient quantity to make an impact upon the poor state of British coinage. Nonetheless, most coins in circulation were hammered pieces, some of which dated back to Tudor times. Despite severe penalties, including death and long prison sentences, there were always those willing to risk clipping away the edges of the old hammered coins.

"During more than thirty years [since milled coinage began] this evil has gone on increasing," noted the historian, Thomas Macaulay. "At first, it had been disregarded, but it had at length become an insupportable curse to the country. It was to no purpose that the rigorously executed. At every session that was held at the Old Bailey terrible examples were made. Hurdles with four, five, six wretches convicted of counterfeiting or mutilating the money of the realm, were dragged month after month up Holborn Hill. On one morning seven men were hanged and a woman burned for clipping."[1]

Did these executions have the desired effect? Macaulay says they did not, and explains why.

'. . . all was in vain," he said. "The gains were such as to lawless spirits seemed more proportional to the risks. Some clippers were said to have made great fortunes. One in particular offered six thousand pounds for a pardon. His bribe was indeed rejected, but the fame of his riches did much to counteract the effect which the spectacle of his death was designed to produce."[2]

The continuing evil of clipping may have been readily apparent to the general public, but it had not made sufficient impact upon either Charles II or James II to stir them to action. However, clipping was to be eliminated from the English scene for all time before the next King, William III, would end his reign. Moreover, he was to accomplish this extraordinary feat not through penalties and punishments, but through legislation and a massive recoinage.

When Mary set foot in England, she had been of two minds. On the one hand, she was proud of her husband, who would become William III, for delivering the country from its state of turmoil. On the other, she never forgot that it was her father, James II, who was the centre of the unrest. ". . . when I saw England, my native country . . .," she wrote in her diary, "I felt a secret joy . . ., but that was soon checked with the consideration of my father's misfortunes which came immediately to my mind."[3] William and Mary were crowned in February of 1689, but it was to be 1692 before the first shilling of the new reign

WILLIAM AND MARY: THE ROYAL ARMS CHANGES
With the accession of William and Mary (above), the royal arms and coin of the realm incorporated the lion of Orange-Nassau (centre, above).

was struck and, indeed, very few of these were issued. The following year, 1693, was the only one for which there would be a normal quantity of shillings struck in the names of the joint sovereigns.

Not since the time of Philip and Mary (1554–8) had the Mint been confronted with the task of placing two busts on the same side of the nation's coinage. Given the tenor of the times, the solution had to be achieved with delicacy. As King, William was expected by some to have the dominant position on the coins. However, he was a foreigner, albeit a Protestant one. Mary, on the other hand, was for others a symbol of the Stuarts. What was to be done?

Conjoined Busts of William and Mary

The engraver solved the dilemma by adopting a style of presentation hitherto unknown of British coins – conjoined busts. He decided to project Mary's profile farther to the right, but to superimpose upon it the bust of William. Thus it could be said that either of the royal personages had been accorded the more prominent position.

Circling the conjoined busts is the legend, GULIELMUS.ET.MARIA. DEI. GRATIA. The reverse of this new shilling presents a striking contrast to the reverses of the coins of James II and Charles II. The joint monarchs are proclaimed in a legend reading REX . ET . REGINA . MAG. BR. FR. ET. HI. The principal design of the reverse is a cross, not unlike those that appeared on the coins of James II and Charles II. Each arm of the cross bears a symbol representing England, Scotland, Ireland and France. In the centre, however, is a device new to British coinage – the lion of Orange-Nassau – in tribute to William's descent from the Dutch royal family. In the angles of the cross is a monogram combining the initials W and M in a most pleasing manner. The final feature of this reverse of William and Mary's shilling is the placing of one numeral of the four-numeral date, 1692 (or 1693), in each of the four angles of the cross.

FIRST CONJOINED BUSTS
William and Mary face to the right on this
1692 shilling. Their coins have the only conjoined busts in the history of British
coinage.

But this coin portraying the royal couple was destined to be short-lived. Mary died from
smallpox in 1694 at the age of 32, leaving the grief-stricken William to continue his royal
obligations alone.

William's Resolve to Improve the Coinage

Perhaps out of proverbial Dutch efficiency and determination, William was unhappy about
the state of Britain's coinage and determined to improve it. A leading historian and
numismatist, the late Sir Charles Oman, has stated that perhaps 52% of Britain's early
currency was clipped,[4] and that the mutilation must have meant a loss of at least one third
of the original silver content. The scandal was the subject of sermons, essays and Parliamentary debates.

Macaulay writes that the clipping abuse grew "with constantly accelerating velocity"
and that by 1695, the year after Queen Mary's death, the country hardly possessed any
coin suitable for trading. "It was," he added, "a mere chance whether what was called a
shilling was really tenpence, sixpence, or a groat."[5] He also tells the story about a man,
known as "an honest Quaker," from the north of England who had unclipped coins which
he used on a journey to the south. ". . . shopkeepers and innkeepers stared at the broad and
heavy halfcrowns with which he paid his way," and, the historian adds, "asked whence he
came, and where such money was to be found."[6]

The passing of bad coins between citizen and trader caused much ill feeling and frequently led to physical abuse. Even the slightest purchase became the subject of dispute.
Wrangling became the way of life, and on the day when the employee paid off his workmen,
heated discussion about the sad state of the coins was inevitable. "On a fair day or a market
day," notes one account, "the clamours, the reproaches, the taunts, the curses, were
incessant, and it was well if no booth was overturned and no head broken."[7]

Severe Penalties for Clipping

Another effect of the appalling coinage was its upward pressure on prices. Whether the consumer made a major purchase, say of a pair of shoes, or merely wanted to pay for his
tankard of ale, the result was the same – a reluctance by the shopkeeper, publican, or
whoever – to accept a mutilated shilling which, in effect, was worth only sixpence. Inform-
ing against clippers sometimes took on Gestapo-like similarities. Forty pounds – more than
two year's wages for the unskilled worker – awaited anyone who informed on a clipper, but
a man already convicted of clipping could obtain a pardon if he informed on two clippers. If
a man was caught in the act of clipping, he knew he might be lucky to escape with his life.
But even to be found in possession of silver filings or parings was enough to subject the
unfortunate person to being burned in the cheek with a red-hot iron.

WINDOW TAX IMPOSED TO RAISE REVENUE FOR RECOINAGE

The tax made possible necessary funds for the recoinage, but brought misery and ill-health to millions for the next century and a half. This *Punch* cartoon depicts the relief of an impoverished family when, in 1850, repeal of the tax was proposed; it was entitled: "Hollo! Old Fellow; We're Glad to See You Here."

William III, ever the practical man, saw that punishment for clipping – however brutal or unjustified – was not effective, and realized a scheme had to be implemented whereby all holders of clipped or mutilated coinage would be guaranteed the original value of the pieces. He knew that such a public assurance would be costly, would take several years to complete and would leave unpunished many of those who had taken part in abusing the coin of the realm. Yet he knew that only such a plan, enforced throughout the land, would ensure that all old coins were turned in for redemption.

If William made a mistake in outlining the scheme, it was in allowing too much time for the public to bring in their poor coins. Assured that any old shilling could be exchanged for a bright new one, everyone rushed to shear even more metal from their already mutilated pieces. But the King needed time to raise money for the recoinage because, once the new coins were in production, the Mint would be swamped with offers of the old clipped pieces. The Mint could not risk running out of funds to finance the new coinage, so some form of

MACAULAY DESCRIBES THE ACTIVITY AT LONDON'S TOWER MINT
The historian, Thomas Macaulay (above, left) recreated the atmosphere of William III's recoinage operation in London. "Every day," he wrote, "huge heaps of pared and defaced crowns and shillings were turned into many ingots which were instantly sent off to the mint in the Tower (right)."

tax had to be devised, with the entire population sharing the burden, that would provide a large sum quickly. But what kind of tax would fit all these requirements?

"It occurred to the Chancellor of the Exchequer," recounts Macaulay, "that it might be possible to devise an impost on houses, which might be not less productive nor less certain than the hearth money, but which might press less heavily on the poor, and might be collected by a less vexatious process. The number of hearths in a house could not be ascertained without domiciliary visits. The windows a collector might count without passing the threshold."[8]

The Sun Obliterated to Improve the Coinage

Thus was born the infamous "window tax," a device that was to remain in effect until the middle of the last century, when it was replaced by the house tax. Today, scattered throughout Britain, are houses dating from the time of William III or earlier with windows bricked up as mute reminders of former occupants' cunning in reducing the amount of tax due.

When the window tax was announced, there was a great rush in the land to brick up windows. However, few families wanted to live in total darkness, and in the end the tax netted more than £1,200,000 – slightly more than was needed to meet the cost of the recoinage. With arrangements complete for calling in the bad coins and a system formulated for raising the required finance, all that remained was the actual task itself. The great question was: could the Tower mint in London produce coins fast enough to enable the population to go about its normal business with a minimum of disruption?

The Mint realized that it could not cope with a swift recoinage operation, and so provincial mints were authorized to supplement the London output. Hastily, but without loss of quality, dies and equipment were moved to Bristol, Chester, Exeter, Norwich and

PROVINCIAL SHILLING
A quarter of William III's new coins were struck in the provinces. Shown are pieces of Bristol and Exeter (top row), Norwich and Exeter (bottom), and Chester in the centre. The initial letters – B, E, C, N and Y are beneath the busts.

York. By the end of 1696, the five provincial mints were operational; the London mint had worked at capacity for the entire year.

Several writers have provided a vivid picture of life in London and the provinces during the period leading up to the recoinage (when clipping was resumed on a frantic scale), and during the actual minting operation. As expected, the London mint was the busiest in the land; "Ten furnaces were erected in the garden behind the Treasury," one historian recorded, "and every day huge heaps of pared and defaced crowns and shillings were turned into many ingots which were instantly sent off to the mint in the Tower."[9]

Each branch mint placed the first letter of the city's name on the coins it struck. In all cases, these letters – B, C, E, N, and Y – were put below the bust of William. Only at York was there a variation; some shillings and other coins bear a capital Y, while others have a small one.

Those who directed the recoinage effort may have congratulated themselves on raising the required cost by the window tax, and on establishing branch mints so that a great deal of coin could be produced in a short time, but the progress of the gigantic operation was not to be as smooth as those in authority had hoped.

The diarist John Evelyn noted in his journal, under the date of February 23rd, 1696, that "they now began to coin new money [in London]." Nearly three months later (May 13th) he wrote: "Money still continuing exceeding scarce, so that none was paid or receiv'd, but all was on trust, the Mint not supplying for common necessities." Even on June 11th the situation was still chaotic. "Want of current money to carry on the smallest concerns, even for daily provisions in the markets," he noted. ". . . nothing considerable coin'd of the new and now only [sic] current stamp, cause such a scarcity that tumults are every day fear'd, no body paying or receiving money; so imprudent was the late Parliament" he added, "to condemn the old [coin], tho' clipt, and corrupted, till they had provided supplies."

Even the ballad singer chronicled the dilemma of a population which had turned in its old money and had not yet received anthing in its place:

> We parted with all our old money to show
> We foolishly hoped for plenty of new,
> But might have remembered when we came to the push
> That a bird in the hand is worth two in the bush.[10]

ST. PETER'S HOSPITAL, SITE OF WILLIAM III'S BRISTOL MINT
Here, from 1696 to 1698, over £455,000 in silver coin was struck, each piece bearing the letter B beneath the King's bust. This building unfortunately was destroyed during the Second World War.

London's Tower mint and the five provincial ones eventually overcame their production problems and slowly the nation's commerce was sated with new coins. As expected, the London mint turned out the bulk of the new pieces, but the smaller mints between them provided 26% of the value of the new coinage – thereby enabling the gigantic task to be completed in a much shorter time than would have been possible with only the London mint in operation. Exeter led the provincial mints in the value of coin struck (£456,000), closely followed by Bristol (£455,000). Chester produced £315,000 in silver, York £306,000, and Norwich £257,000. Total value of the silver recoinage was £6,882,000 of which the London mint struck £5,091,000 and the five provincial mints together, £1,791,000.

Celia Fiennes, the diarist, observed the recoinage effort at York. "I saw them at work," she wrote, "and stamp'd one halfe crown my self; they dispatch worke very fast and have coyn'd several 1000 L. I see all parts of the work about – the pounding the boyling refineing

TOWER MINT SHILLING

This William III shilling was struck at the Tower mint two years before the King died after a riding accident.

and makeing Barres and cutting out in the mill and bakeing and stamping – all but Milling which art they are sworne to keep private."[11]

In Bristol, recoinage was welcomed as much as in any other place in the land for, as one chronicler put it, the state of silver coin was "miserably bad." In 1695 a number of clippers and counterfeit coiners had been discovered and some of the offenders were committed to Gloucester and others to Newgate. One Mrs. Scarlett was condemned to be burned at the stake, but was reprieved and eventually escaped. Bristol's mint began working in September, 1696, in the sugar-house behind St. Peter's Church. Here, an historian records, "our mint coined £2000 some weeks . . . so that new money came about sooner than was expected . . . ."[12]

A Shilling Punched Through

An interesting variety of mutilated coin circulated for about a year (November, 1695 to November, 1696) during the recoinage operation. Old hammered pieces, some no doubt dating back to the Tudor reigns, were allowed to pass as legal tender provided (a) they were not much clipped and (b) they had been punched through the middle "with a solid punch that shall make a hole without Diminishing the Silver." Such punched coins were allowed to circulate at full face value (i.e., by *tale*) during the time when the several mints were struggling to turn out the new pieces of William III. An ordinary nail seems to have been used for punching through some of these coins. Very few survive, for in the generations since they circulated, the public mistakenly took them to be worth only their silver content, and thus most have disappeared into melting pots.[13] It was one such shilling that Joseph Addison described in his essay, "Adventures of a Shilling," that appeared in *The Tatler* (for the full text of this essay, see "The Chronicles" toward the end of this work).

The last four years of William's reign saw the return on British coins of two provenance marks: the plumes to denote silver from Welsh mines and the rose for coins made from West of England silver. During 1698–1699 there appeared a coin with an interesting variety of the King's bust. This type, portraying William's hair flowing across the top of his head, came to be known as the "flaming hair" variety. William died in 1702 at the relatively young age of fifty-four after a riding accident.

Queen Anne: the Last Stuart Monarch

Princess Anne, as the sister of Mary II, had willingly surrendered her right to the British throne to William so that he could be monarch in his own right. When Anne assumed the throne in 1702 at the age of 37, she became the fourth woman to grace the shillings of Britain.

During Anne's reign the shilling and other denominations recorded deeds at home and abroad. In addition, provenance marks still denoted the origin of metallic content. There

QUEEN ANNE: VIGO COIN
Less than a year after the Queen (left) ascended the throne, enough bullion was captured from a Spanish treasure fleet in Vigo Bay to permit striking of nearly £100,000 in shillings and other denominations. Note VIGO under the bust.

was also another shilling bearing the letter E to denote the place of minting, but unlike the E in William III's reign which represented Exeter, this time it stood for the Scottish mint at Edinburgh. Altogether, Anne's brief reign of a dozen years provides a rich variety of shillings to document events of her time.

Booty Provides Shillings Marked VIGO

In the very first year of her rule, a daring attack in Spain's Bay of Vigo led to a victory and capture of bullion that resulted in shillings and other coins being marked VIGO. The adventure got under way after the British and Dutch heard rumours that a Spanish treasure fleet had just arrived in the Bay of Vigo from the West Indies. The Spanish thought that the bay would provide effective concealment for the richly laden vessels, but this strategy proved to be wrong.

The two allies quickly assembled a fleet of fifty ships and, despite encountering French men-of-war and frigates positioned to protect the Spanish treasure vessels, the invading ships sailed into the bay. In the action that followed, the British and Dutch overran the enemy's sea and land defences and captured or destroyed thirty-seven French and Spanish vessels. This was a major blow to the combined enemy fleet, but the triumph also gave the victors a handsome fortune in goods and bullion.

The value of the silver taken is reputed to have been several hundred thousand pounds, but by the time the treasure was divided among all those having a claim to some of it, only about £95,000 worth reached the British Treasury. Nonetheless, the quantity was sufficient to strike a series of coins in silver – among them the shilling – which bear the word VIGO beneath Queen Anne's bust. The silver reached the Mint in time for only a few coins of 1702 to be struck with the VIGO mark, but all those issued in 1703 have the distinctive word on them. Responsibility for producing the VIGO coins fell on Isaac Newton, who had been named mintmaster in 1699.

Whereas William III faces to the right on his coins, Anne faces left. The obverse of the

ROSES AND PLUMES

This shilling, struck the year before Queen Anne died, bears roses and plumes, alternately positioned, in the angles of the reverse.

Queen's shillings changed little during her reign, the major exceptions being the addition of provenance marks. Although Anne is reported to have been annoyed at the low neckline of her bust on the shilling and other coins, this feature was left unchanged except on certain gold pieces where she is more fully clothed.

If the obverses of the Queen's shilling showed little change during her reign, the same cannot be said for the reverses. The first change was the deletion of William III's Dutch symbol, the lion of Orange-Nassau in the centre of the cross. This was replaced with the star of the Order of the Bath. Two provenance marks, the Welsh plumes and a combination of plumes and roses, appeared on shillings of Anne for most of her reign. These were attractively positioned in the angles of the cross on the reverse; the plumes device occurs on shillings dated 1702, 1704–5, and 1707–8, while the roses and plumes were featured on shillings dated 1705, 1707–8, 1710, and 1712–14.

One of the most significant events of Anne's reign was the formal union of Scotland with England. This occasion was appropriately recorded on coins of the realm by changing the heraldic devices on the reverse. Before the Act of Union, separate arms of the cross had borne the symbols of the two countries. Now the leopards of England and the rampant lion of Scotland found themselves within the same heraldic "zoo" on two of the four arms of the cross, with the French and Irish symbols on the remaining pair.

In 1714 Queen Anne died, leaving no issue. The long and difficult period of the Stuart dynasty was at last over. Under the Stuarts the nation had faced its gravest crisis since Tudor times, and at one stage the monarchy itself had been deposed. But the realm had survived and, under Anne, was strengthened when Scotland formally became a part of the United Kingdom.

VII
Enter the Hanoverians

"The long passages hung with buckets, appended, in idle row, to walls, whose substance might defy any, short of the last, conflagration: — with vast ranges of cellarage under all, where dollars and pieces-of-eight once lay, an "unsunned heap," for Mammon to have solaced his solitary heart withal, — long since dissipated or scattered into air at the blast of the break-ing of that famous bubble . . .. Such is the SOUTH-SEA HOUSE."

From the *Essays of Elia*, by Charles Lamb.

Under the Act of Settlement (1701) Britain turned to the Continent to find a successor to Queene Anne. He was George Louis, the Elector of Hanover, who became George I. When he arrived in Britain, he spoke virtually no English. He reigned for thirteen years, but took only a passing interest in national affairs and made little effort to learn English. His heart remained in Hanover, where he was immensely popular, and he visited there regularly throughout his years as King.

The Sovereign of Many Titles

The transition from the Stuart dynasty to the Hanoverian line brought dramatic changes in the appearance of the shilling. Apart from the profile of a new monarch (George was fifty-four when he ascended the throne), the shilling attempted to list all the British and German titles of the King. To spell these out in full would have proved impossible in the space available. The King's British titles had to state DEI GRATIA MAGNAE BRITANNIAE, FRANCIAE ET HIBERNIAE REX FIDEI DEFENSOR, while his German ones were even longer: BRUNSVICENSIS ET LUNEBERGENSIS DUX, SACRI ROMANI IMPERII ARCHITHESAURARIUS ET ELECTOR.

Even putting the British legend on one side of the coin and the German ones on the other would not solve the problem: the wording was just too long. The only solution was to abbreviate the titles. Thus, George I's shillings read, around his profile, D.G.M.BR.FR.ET HIB.REX F.D., and on the reverse, BRUN.ET L.DUX S.R.I.A. TH. ET EL. (taking both sides together, the abbreviations translate into "By the Grace of God, King of Great Britain, France, and Ireland, Defender of the Faith; Duke of Brunswick and Luneburg, High Treasurer and Elector of the Holy Roman Empire"). No wonder one observer commented at the time that the legend, being expressed only in abbreviations or initials, had become virtually unintelligible.

Apart from bearing the monarch's lengthy title, the shillings of George I have on their reverses strikingly different devices from those of the preceding Stuart sovereigns. Just as William III installed the lion of Orange-Nassau on his shillings, so George I now introduced the arms of the Electorate of Hanover on his coins. A cross on the reverse allots separate bars to Ireland and France, but relegates England to sharing a bar with Scotland. The arms of Hanover are on the fourth bar of the cross.

The heraldic device of Hanover is a menagerie in miniature, and to compress all its

72

GEORGE I: SSC SHILLING
The King (left) ruled only 13 years but his reign produced shillings and other denominations marked SSC for the South Sea Company – centre of a great speculative "bubble" in 1720. The SSC shilling is shown above.

details into the small shield allotted for the purpose must have been an engraver's nightmare. One third of the shield has a pair of leopards representing Brunswick, another the rampant lion of Luneberg, and the third a galloping horse of Saxony. In the centre is the crown of Charlemagne, symbolizing the King's office of High Treasurer of the Holy Roman Empire.

Distrust of an heir was to become a marked characteristic of Hanoverian rulers. When George I made his frequent trips to Germany, he was reluctant to leave the Prince of Wales in authority. The Prince had very little to do, and the chasm which had developed between his father and himself soon became permanent. Fortunately, the King's long absences from Britain forced the development of a constitutional device – the cabinet, which could meet without the monarch being present. Robert Walpole became the nation's first Prime Minister under this arrangement in 1721, just in time to help "clear up" the greatest speculative scandal of the century – the famous "South Sea Bubble."

The South Sea Company was formed in 1711 to trade in the South Seas, but soon found itself in the public eye for totally different reasons. It loaned millions of pounds to the government and, while doing so, issued thousands of public shares. Public confidence in the company rose to unrealistic heights, and speculation in South Sea Company shares, as well as in shares of many newly formed companies, was great. Whereas investors today have access to a great deal of information about business firms and can make some judgment of their worth, people who lived in the time of George I knew literally nothing about the companies with whom they were investing. In spite of this alarming dearth of information, large numbers of people flocked to buy shares with only hearsay and rumour to support their action.

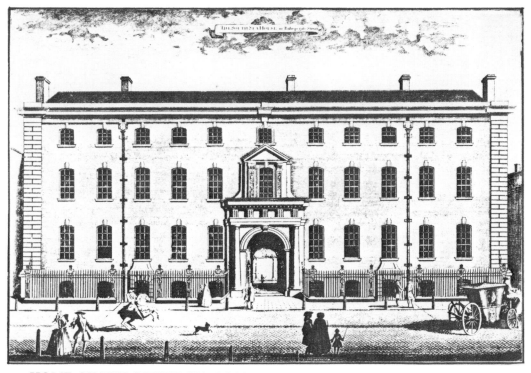

HOME OF THE SOUTH SEA COMPANY
This illustration, taken from *Stone's Survey*, depicts South Sea house in 1754 when the company's shillings had been in circulation for 31 years.

A Time of Widespread Speculation

Not that these foolish citizens were not warned; they were – by the journals of the time, by writers, and even by some statesmen. One verse which circulated widely cautioned against speculation:

> A wise man laughed to see an ass
> Eat thistles and neglect good grass,
> But had the sage beheld the folly
> Of late transacted in Change Alley
> He might have seen worse asses there
> Give solid gold for empty air.

Eventually the South Sea Company itself became concerned by the frenzied trading. Then some of the smaller firms foundered and collapsed. The public rushed to sell and the speculative "bubble" was pricked. The rapid sell-off of South Sea Company shares and those of lesser known firms, was disastrous for those who had held on to their securities. In the month of September, 1720, South Sea Company shares plummeted from 1,000 to 175.

HOGARTH'S REPRESENTATION OF THE SOUTH SEA "BUBBLE"

Many of Britain's most prominent citizens lost fortunes when the South Sea "bubble" burst in 1720. The event led William Hogarth to sketch this brilliant satire on the speculative nature of his contemporaries.

The list of those who suffered heavy losses reads like a "Who's Who" of the period. As often happens in speculation, those engaged in the professions suffered most; Jonathan Swift and Alexander Pope were among them, as well as the noted portrait painter, Sir Godfrey Kneller. John Gay, who wrote *The Beggar's Opera*, originally counted himself to be a lucky man when he bought shares at what seemed a good price, but he subsequently ignored the advice of friends to sell and wound up with a heavy loss. Many of the great men who saw their life's savings suddenly disappear were bitter about their misfortune, and Alexander Pope did not hesitate to put his own feelings in print in a biting satire, his *Epistle to Allen, Lord Bathurst*:

> At length corruption, like a general flood
> Did deluge all, and avarice creeping on
> Spread like a low-born mist and hid the sun.
> Statesmen and patriots plied alike the stocks,

Peeress and butler shared alike the box,
And judges jobbed and bishops bit the town,
And mighty dukes packed cards for half-a-crown –
Britain was sunk in lucre's sordid charms.

South Sea Company (SSC) Shillings

Because it was the most prominent of the firms involved, the South Sea Company became
the subject of an enquiry led by Sir Robert Walpole. In his findings, many figures
prominent in government were discovered to have taken part in the dealings. But the
Company survived the scandal and continued to trade overseas in the normal way. Among
the places where it operated was the west coast of South America, including Peru, where
considerable quantities of silver were obtained. Some of the silver bullion from South
America was required to be sent to the mint as a kind of reparation after the speculative
scandal.[1] Shillings, as well as crowns, halfcrowns, and sixpences, were struck in 1723
bearing the initials of the Company on their reverses. The bullion provided by the South
Sea Company was large enough to provide most of the nation's silver coinage in 1723. Thus
a company which had seen its name associated with the most publicized speculation in
modern times lived on to see its initials grace the coin of the realm.

The provenance mark used most often on shillings of George I is the roses and plumes
device, indicating mixed silver from the West of England and Wales. This combination
symbol appears on shillings dated for every year of the King's reign, except the first. There
was also a tiny trickle of silver being mined by the Welsh Copper Company; coins struck in
this silver have the initials W.C.C. beneath the bust of George I, and on the reverse the
Welsh plumes alternate with an attractive double-C monogram in the angles of the cross.
Since so few W.C.C. shillings were struck, they are among the rarest of this reign.

To George I's reign belongs credit for incorporating one royal title that had been little
used since it was first granted to Henry VIII, that of FIDEI DEFENSOR (Defender of the
Faith). Until then no one had thought of placing it on British coinage; with its introduction
on the shillings and other pieces of George I, it was to remain a part of the monarch's title.
The sole exception, which did not affect shillings, occurs on the famous "Godless Florin" of
Queen Victoria dated 1849.

George I died in 1727 during one of his periodic visits to Hanover, and was buried there.
He was the last British sovereign to be interred abroad. On his death the crown passed to
his only son who became George II.

Although George II kept his German titles on his shillings and other coins, he was far
more interested in the affairs of Britain than his father had been. He mastered the English
language, took a degree from Cambridge, and his love of music led George Frederick
Handel to take up residence in England.

George II's Shillings: the End of Provenance Marks

Shillings of George II are divided easily into two types insofar as the King's bust is concerned. The first coin portrays the monarch's "young head," the second series, the "old."
The young head types were struck as late as 1741, and the old head variety began in 1743.
But it is not the bust types that constitute the main interest in George II's shillings;
provenance marks now appeared for the last time – one of them involving a dramatic
adventure at sea.

GEORGE II: LIMA SHILLING
In the reign of George II (right) Britain had its second issue of shillings in a generation from coin captured abroad. This time Admiral George Anson led an expedition which brought in £500,000 of specie from Lima's port (Paita) and a treasure ship en route to Manilla.

ANSON'S VICTORY BROUGHT ONE OF HISTORY'S GREATEST PRIZES
Admiral Anson sailed for more than three years chasing Spanish treasure ships. His greatest exploit came off Macao in June, 1743, when his "Centurion" defeated a galleon (above) carrying £445,000 in piastres. This, together with a much smaller sum taken in Peru, allowed the mint to strike half a million pounds worth of gold and silver pieces, all of which were marked LIMA.

Silver became scarce not only in Britain, but worldwide. The price rose sharply, resulting in very little silver coinage being struck. Between 1727 and 1751 only £227,000 worth was coined. Had it not been for the daring capture of booty by Admiral George Anson during more than three years of treasure-seeking, the value of coins struck during the 24-year period would have been halved. Anson seized some of his loot in the Peruvian port of Paita, near Lima, and more from a treasure ship making its annual voyage from Acapulco, Mexico, to Manila. When he returned to Spithead in June, 1744, with his cargo of precious metal, he was promptly made Rear Admiral and given other honours. To mark the happy windfall of bullion at a time when it was sorely needed, the Mint placed the word LIMA beneath the bust of George II's shillings dated 1745 and 1746, as well as on some other pieces of silver and gold.

Silver from Britain's own mines continued to find its way to the mint, but in ever-diminishing amounts. Two old provenance marks long identified with British sources of silver now made their valedictory appearance: the roses indicating West of England mines and the combined roses and plumes signifying bullion from Wales.

George II died in 1760 at the age of 76. He was the last British sovereign to be buried at Westminster Abbey. As none of his sons survived him, the crown passed to his grandson, who became George III.

The worldwide shortage of silver continued in the reign of George III, and for the first twenty-seven years of his rule no shillings appeared except two very small, but remarkable issues.

A Shilling for the Lord Lieutenant of Ireland

The first, known today as the "Northumberland shilling," was a public relations coup that would have been the envy of today's promoters. These coins take their name from the Earl of Northumberland who was appointed Lord Lieutenant of Ireland and while there, passed out a small quantity of George III shillings that had been especially struck for him. For many years it was assumed that the Earl had the shillings struck *before* going to Dublin to take up his appointment and that on arrival, he went ceremoniously through the streets tossing out the shiny new pieces of his sovereign to onlookers. Recent research indicates that the coins were not struck until approximately six months after the Earl's appointment, and that any largesse was restricted to giving friends and new acquaintances coins, one or two at the time.

But the story of the Northumberland shilling does not end here, for the issuance of the coin by the Earl tells a great deal about the aristocrat and his wife, and the times they lived in. Hugh Percy became Earl of Northumberland in 1749 and eventually became a favourite of George II. In 1753 he was named Lord of the Bedchamber and three years later was awarded the Order of the Garter. When George III came to the throne, he was again named Lord of the Bedchamber. In 1762 he became Lord Chamberlain to Queen Charlotte.

Northumberland's popularity with the royal families left him with both enemies and admirers. An exceedingly handsome man and possessed of great personal charm, he was regarded by some as an opportunist. Among those who shared this view was Horace Walpole, who made no secret of his dislike of the man. "With the mechanic [al] application to every branch of knowledge, he possessed none beyond the surface," wrote Walpole. He added that "the old nobility beheld his pride with envy and anger, and thence were the less disposed to overlook the littleness of his temper."[2]

GEORGE III: FIRST SHILLING
The reign of George III (right) was marked by Britain's involvement in foreign wars, which contributed to the high cost of silver and a dearth of silver coin. The only coin struck when the King was a young man (he was 25 at the time) was this "Northumberland shilling" (1763).

Louis Dutens, a Swiss-born clergyman who later became secretary to the Earl, was in a much better position to judge Northumberland; he described him as having "great talents and more knowledge than is generally found amongst the nobility." He went on to say that the Earl's expenditures "were unexampled in his time, he was not generous, but passed for being so owing to his judicious manner of bestowing favours."[3]

The Countess of Northumberland also felt the venom of Walpole's pen. She was fond of the high society of her day, leading the author to describe her as "junketaceous;" he also credited her with an excess of "patrician pride and ostentation." He added that the Countess much delighted in following the Queen to London theatres with a retinue longer than the royal one. While pretending to be frank, she was – Walpole would have us believe – simply being mischievous.

Thanks to Walpole, we have a vivid description of the lady's love of pageantry and her ability to mix with citizens of all ranks. "The Countess . . .," he said, "was a jovial heap of contradictions. The blood of all the Percies and Seymours swelled in her veins and in her fancy, while her person was more vulgar than anything but her conversation, which was larded indiscriminately with her stories of her ancestors and her footmen." Then Walpole portrayed the Countess in action. "Show and crowds and junketing were her endless pursuits," he said. "She was familiar with the mob while stifled with diamonds, and yet was attentive to the most minute privileges of her rank while almost shaking hands with a cobbler . . .. She had revived the drummers and pipers and obsolete minstrels of her family, and her own buxom countenance at the tail of such a procession gave it all the air of an antiquated pageant or mumming."[4]

The Countess Admired by Goldsmith and Boswell

Dutens, who saw a great deal of the Countess, strongly defended her behaviour. While agreeing she had a strong attachment to her views, he added that she was possessed of great magnanimity. Other contemporaries seemed to have been impressed with, if not smitten by

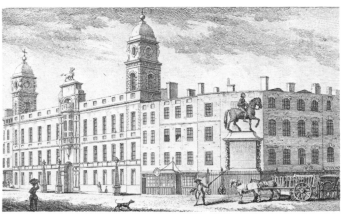

THE DUCHESS: NORTHUMBERLAND HOUSE
Elizabeth, Duchess of Northumberland (left) organized
sparkling social functions at Northumberland House
(above). A collector of medals, she may have inspired the
striking of the "Northumberland shilling." Wits used to
tell visitors to Northumberland House that the Percy lion
on the roof, if stared at closely, could be seen to wag its
tail.

her. Goldsmith composed for her his ballad, "Edwin and Angelina," and Boswell considered himself highly complimented by having exchanged correspondence with her. She was also an able hostess at Northumberland House where her sparkling social events – often enlivened by the performance of leading musicians – were the talk of London.

It must have come as no surprise to their friends that the Earl was chosen to be Lord Lieutenant of Ireland in April of 1763. Christopher Smart wasted no time in writing an "Ode to the Earl of Northumberland on his being appointed Lord Lieutenant of Ireland." One verse of this work will suffice to illustrate the esteem with which the poet held his hero:

> In pity to our sister isle
> With sighs we lend thee for a while;
>   O be thou soon restor'd,
> Tho' Stanhope, Halifax were there,
> We never had a man to spare
>   Our love could less afford.[5]

The Northumberland Shilling: Brainchild of the Countess?

Christopher Smart was not the only person who took the initiative to mark the beginning of Northumberland's assignment to Ireland. Someone, and there is some basis for believing it was the Countess, thought of having the Mint strike new shillings which the Lord Lieutenant could distribute while in Dublin. This fascinating lady is known to have been a

THE DUKE'S MEDAL
The Duke of Northumberland (below), as seen on a medal struck in 1766 to commemorate the restoration of Alnwick Castle.

ALNWICK CASTLE: HOME OF THE DUKE
This formidable Border fortress has been the seat of the Percy family since Norman times. Its first major restoration was undertaken in the time of George III after the Duke had served as Lord Lieutenant of Ireland – a period which saw his "Northumberland shilling" issued.

collector and an authority on medals. She employed Dutens, who frequently travelled to the Continent, as her agent in acquiring medals and coins for her collection. In time her collection grew to many hundreds and it survived intact until the 1980s when it was sold in two stages by a well known London auction house.[6] Given the Countess' vast knowledge of coins and medals and the appeal which they held for her, it seems quite likely that the notion of striking new shillings for her husband's Dublin assignment was her own or, at very least, enjoyed her support. By coincidence, the Mint had already started work on a new issue of shillings for George III, although the dies were not ready until September of 1763.

Mint records show that 48 pounds of the George III shillings were struck in 1763. At standard weight, this would have permitted 2,976 "Northumberland" pieces to be made. Thanks to the initiative of the Earl (or his wife), the nation gained its only shilling with a youthful bust of George III. It was not until 1787, when the King was almost fifty, that his next shilling would appear.

At least one of Northumberland's retainers received the new shillings while in the Lord Lieutenant's service in Dublin. Edward Hawkins (1780–1867), noted numismatist and keeper of antiquaries at the British Museum, recorded that he acquired three or four examples from the person who had been Northumberland's Dublin housekeeper.[7] Certainly most of the coins were carefully put away, for almost all that turn up today are in excellent condition.

The Northumberlands' last years were spent restoring Alnwick Castle to its former spendour. By now they enjoyed the titles of Duke and Duchess and it seems, out of a sense

COINAGE 27 YEARS LATE
George III came to the throne in 1760, but it was not until 1787 that a shilling and other values were struck in quantity.

of pride to the ancient House of Percy that they were content to concentrate on bringing the castle back to the standard it once enjoyed. "[The Duke] . . . completely rebuilt it," records a confidant of the family, "and out of complaisance to the Duchess, his lady, ornamented it in the Gothic style which he himself did not like, but he did it with so much taste that he made it one of the most superb buildings of that kind in Europe." Meanwhile, the Duke and the Duchess continued their several avocations. "I was dazzled by the magnificence of the Duke," said his trusted advisor, "enchanted by the politeness and attention with which he honoured me . . . . The Duke was fond of the arts and sciences." Of the Duchess' attributes the confidant had this to say: "[She] . . . was pleased with little witticisms in a circle of friends, and amused herself by collecting prints and medals, and by making collections of different sorts."[8]

As for the shilling itself, there is not a word on it to document its association with Northumberland's service as Lord Lieutenant of Ireland.

A Few Shillings for Christmas

In 1787 the price of silver declined slightly and the Bank of England ordered £55,280 in new coins from the Mint. The Bank did not have the general public in mind (if it had, a much larger sum in coins would have been ordered); instead, the shiny new pieces were intended for distribution to its customers in small quantities at Christmas. Even this plan was followed reluctantly and with delay, because the coins had been struck at a loss and as fast as they were distributed, they disappeared into the melting pot. More than a decade later, in 1798, the Bank reported it still had on hand £22,800 of the 1787 coins.[9]

The King, by the time the 1787 coins appeared, had taken on the appearance of an old man, in real life as well as on his money, for by now he was increasingly beset with physical and mental illness. His bust on the 1787 shilling, compared with that on the Northumberland piece, shows a man much fuller in face, and with a receding hairline. Artistically, the 1787 coin is a great improvement over the rather austere shillings of the preceding Hanoverians, George I and George II.

There are two major varieties of the 1787 shilling – a "hearts" type, and a "no hearts" type. This unusual distinction arises from the difference in one of the four small shields on the shilling's reverse. The shield with the variation is that representing Hanover which bears the rampant lion of Luneberg. One variety has a sprinkling of hearts around the lion, and the other does not. Neither type is particularly scarce.

The Shilling that was Recalled

In 1798 one of the most bizarre transactions in the history of the Mint occurred. Since August of the previous year the market price of silver had dropped below the Mint price. It

DORRIEN AND MAGENS TYPE
This 1798 George III shilling was struck
and then withdrawn, to the dismay of
London bankers.

was then legal for firms and individuals to take bullion to the Mint to have it made into
coins. Ten bankers decided, given the favourable price of silver, to have a quantity of shillings struck, for this denomination was that most desired by the public.

The bankers intended to have massive quantities of shillings struck and, between April
and July, sent just over £30,000 to the Mint – a sum that would have provided in excess of
600,000 pieces. The Mint began striking the new pieces in anticipation of making the first
delivery on May 16, but a week before this date – when more than half of the money had
been partly coined – the Privy Council Committee on Coin ordered the Mint to halt its
work until the attitude of Parliament could be determined. The order reflected the concern
of the Committee over the Government's inability to produce silver coins at a time when the
price of silver was unstable, and even new standards of silver content in coins were under
consideration. Put bluntly, the order to halt the striking of the bankers' shillings was a
device to borrow time until the issues involved could be more fully discussed. Even so, the
cessation order was illegal and it took an act of Parliament in June to regularize the Committee's wishes.

The bankers, although paid in Exchequer bills for their silver, were furious. Meanwhile,
the remaining silver bullion went to the Bank of England, and the Mint held the shillings
already struck until July, 1799. This interval was long enough for some pieces to go astray,
although the issue remains one of the rarest of the shilling series.[10]

THE SHILLING TOKENS OF THE 1790s
In the last decade of the eighteenth century many thousands
of copper tokens, mostly farthings, halfpennies and pennies,
were struck to alleviate the shortage of small change. A few
places also issued tokens of higher denominations, among
them shillings. Perhaps the most attractive of these are the
Basingstoke Canal shilling pictured here, and Dundee's shillings which were struck in silver (see the chapter on Scottish
shillings). Other eighteenth century shilling tokens were
issued for Epping Forest (1796) and Birmingham (1798).

One banker, Magens Dorrien Magens, did not take the coinage defeat lightly. He loudly proclaimed he had been victimized and circulated pamphlets outlining his grievances. As he was the most vociferous objector to the melting down of the 1798 shillings, those few pieces that escaped have come to be known as the "Dorrien and Magens" variety. Just as with the Northumberland shilling, the Dorrien and Magens type has no distinguishing feature associating it with the parties who instigated the issue. The 1798 shilling is actually an updated example of the 1787 coin. The new date, 1798, is substituted, the small dot which appeared above the King's bust on the 1787 issue is omitted, and the legend on the reverse is in slightly larger letters. There are also minute differences in the bust.

When the eighteenth century ended George III had been on the throne for forty years. Yet this long period saw only a single general issue of shillings, plus the remarkable pieces struck for Northumberland and Dorrien and Magens.

VIII
A Silver Token Revolution

". . . I believe that I may assert that in no part of the country, except where local tokens have been issued, there have been found a permanent plenty and sufficiency of silver for all purposes of change and small payments."

J. B. Monck, Member of Parliament for Reading, 1812.

Although George III reigned for 40 years before the eighteenth century came to an end, his government ignored the nation's need for small change, with the single exception of a general issue in 1787. By 1811 matters were much worse. The small amount of previously identifiable coin was now badly worn, this coming at a time when the population showed a sharp increase and when families were on the move to towns and cities.

The ministers of state, preoccupied with the Napoleonic Wars and unable to rely on the traditional sources of cheap silver bullion, preferred to ignore the growing dilemma of the consumer and trader. Their common need was small change, particularly shillings, but London showed not the slightest trace of concern. The high price of silver caused most people to hoard the few good coins in circulation; those that remained became so worn that it was sometimes impossible to tell whose the royal bust was, or the year in which the piece was struck.

That the vast majority of the people still conducted their daily lives with the shilling as their principal medium of exchange is illustrated by a brief reference to wages and the price of essential foods. Bricklayers in the North of England earned 22 shillings a week, but shoemakers were content to receive a third less. Unskilled labourers made 15 shillings, but handloom operators took home only 13 shillings after a week's sweating in the mill. In hamlets and on farms the pay was even less; some agricultural workers counted themselves lucky if they earned more than a shilling a day.

But what could such wages purchase? In 1810, bread sold for 3¾d per pound, and butter 1/1¼d. Cheese, if the labourer wanted it badly enough, took the better part of a day's wage at 8d per pound. With the shilling clearly the most needed coin to cope both with wages and trade, it was small wonder that banker, merchant, and worker alike lived in daily consternation. Some merchants charged a fee of five per cent, or more, for changing a pound note.

A Daring Idea Evolves

Slowly the notion of striking local tokens in silver began to evolve. Most people who considered the matter felt that an issue of minor denominations – farthings, halfpennies, and pennies – would not solve the problem. The country had known such tokens before, mainly in copper, and in former times they had sufficient purchasing power to render them useful in commerce. But wars and the Industrial Revolution had brought about inflation and what the country most needed to stimulate trade was a sufficiency of small change – mainly sixpences and shillings.

SCARCITY OF CHANGE—The total disappearance of Good Coin and the extreme difficulty of procuring Silver Change, continue to perplex, if not to alarm, every description of persons. The Bank [of England] Tokens have been so sparingly issued, that they have hitherto served rather to gratify curiosity than to administer to public convenience. In fact, unless some means are immediately adopted to remedy this daily . . .[increasing] evil, it will be impossible to execute the ordinary transactions of trade. The want of change is no longer merely an inconvenience, but a source of actual distress to thousands of traders and poor people; the former of whom are reduced to the alternative of giving credit, which they wish to avoid, or keeping their commodities in hand; and the latter are compelled to submit to purchases in which the liberty of choice is sacrificed to the necessity of the occasion. It is a serious fact, that several butchers and market people, on the last Taunton market day, declared their intention of withholding all supplies which were not indispensably required by their regular customers, while others avowed their determination to abstain from attending the market altogether.

A SITUATION ALL TOO COMMON THROUGHOUT BRITAIN

This news item originally appeared in the *Taunton Chronicle* in the summer of 1811, and was reproduced by newspapers in Bristol. Similar articles were published elsewhere as the universal shortage of silver change more and more affected trading.

Many people would have remembered the copper tokens in the last decade of the previous century, but most of these were either halfpennies or pennies and would do little to meet the pressing need for coins of higher denominations. Thus a few small traders, country bankers and others now considered issuing tokens in silver – and of useful denominations – provided they could be sure of immunity from prosecution by the government. Minting coins was a monopoly of the state, although twice before the public had issued tokens successfully. Now, however, merchants contemplated issuing not copper tokens of minor denominations, but tokens in silver to take the place of coin of the realm. The paramount question was: would the government step in and prosecute the local token issuers, or would it simply look the other way?

No one could be sure, but there was a ray of hope. As early as 1797 the government – concerned over the scarcity of silver coins – had counter-stamped Spanish dollars. These coins, bearing a small bust of George III stamped upon the portrait of Charles III (or IV) of Spain, were tokens – strictly speaking. In 1804 the government moved to fill the growing need for silver change by authorizing another issue of counter-marked Spanish dollars, this time with a larger and octagonal-shaped stamp. This stamp was taken from that employed on the Maundy pennies and its larger size made for easier identification by the public. Neither the 1797 issue (valued at 4s. 9d.) nor the 1804 specimens (valued at 5s. each) satisfied the public, because of varying sizes, and counterfeiting was rampant. The Bank of England attempted to give these pieces a more official appearance by calling them in and having Matthew Boulton's private mint overstamp them with the bust and title of George III on one side and the figure of Britannia on the other. Helpful though these issues were, they contributed little toward satisfying the public demand for denominations of smaller value.[1]

Eventually (in mid-1811) the government relented and openly went into the token business, issuing Bank of England silver tokens in two denominations – 3s. and 1s. 6d. The Bank's primary reason for choosing these unusual denominations was to differentiate them from coin of the realm;[2] in fact, the words BANK TOKEN on their reverses accomplished

A CHICHESTER LANDMARK
The city's Market Cross (left), as seen in an old print, is depicted on a shilling token (above, enlarged) issued in 1811 by four firms.

this. Thus the public again lost a chance to have the shillings and sixpences so urgently needed. Exasperation grew when traders often found themselves unable to provide change for a pound note with mostly 3s. and 1s. 6d. tokens in the till. Nonetheless, coins of these odd denominations were turned out in vast quantities – about 10 million of the higher value and nearly half that amount of the smaller one.

Meanwhile, merchants round Britain were evolving their own solution. Although Dublin had silver tokens in 1804 and Guernsey issued one in 1809, it was not until the spring of 1811 that traders, bankers and others mustered enough courage to circulate silver tokens in their respective villages and towns. Tradesmen in some places either forgot or deliberately omitted the year of issue on their tokens. Of those which are dated, that of Neath seems to have been the first to be struck in Great Britain. This town issued both shillings and sixpences dated March 11, 1811, as well as some undated pieces. The obverse of the March 11 token bears the town's arms while the reverse has an unusual inscription, NEATH SILVER MEDAL – probably a term meant to head off any official complaint about the legitimacy of the coins. No names of issuers appear on the March 11 Neath tokens, but they are believed to have been issued by Hopkins Rees, a draper, and one D. Morgan, an iron-monger.

Nearly 100 Places Issue Silver Tokens

England's first shilling tokens may have been issued at Shaftesbury by a local bank which was licensed on March 14, 1811. Gradually "token fever" gripped most of England and

PLACE-NAMES ON THE 1811–12 SILVER TOKENS

Although about 100 towns and cities in England and Wales issued silver tokens during 1811–12, the number of place-names appearing on these pieces is much greater because the coins were sometimes intended to circulate in adjacent towns or counties. One Derby shilling, for example, lists six other towns in whose inns the coin was accepted. In the West Country another shilling bears the names of Devon, Cornwall, Barnstaple and Stratton. This comprehensive list, therefore, reveals the large extent to which silver tokens circulated and thereby alleviated public distress.

Alford	Douglas	Lynn	Scarborough
Andover	Dublin	Manchester	Shaftesbury
Ashbourn	Durham	Mansfield	Sheffield
Attleborough	Epworth	March	Shoreham
Barnsley	Essex	Marlborough	Somerset
Barnstaple	Exeter	Merthyr Tydvil	Southampton
Bath	Fazeley	Montgomeryshire	South Wales
Bedworth (Mill)	Flintshire	Nantwich	Stafford
Bilston	Folkestone	Neath	Steyning
Birmingham	From Selwood	Needham Market	Stockport
Blandford	Gainsborough	Newark	Stockton
Bradford	Gloucester	Newcastle-on-	Stratton
Brecknock	Gloucestershire	Tyne	Suffolk
Bridlington	Godalming	Newport, IOW	Swansea
Bridlington Quay	Gosport	Norfolk	Taunton
Brighton	Hampshire	Northampton	Teignmouth
Bristol	Haverfordwest	North Cornwall	Thirsk
Buckinghamshire	Hereford	North Lopham	Trowbridge
Burton	High Wycombe	Northumberland	Wales
Carmarthen	Holbeach	North Wales	Warwickshire
Chard	Ipswich	Nottingham	Welch Principality
Cheltenham	Isle of Wight	Notts	Welshpool
Chesterfield	Launceston	Peterborough	West Riding
Chichester	Leeds	Plymouth	Weybridge
Cornwall	Leicester	Poole	Whitby
Dawley	Lincoln	Portsea	Wiltshire
Derby	Lincolnshire	Portsmouth	Woodbridge
Devon	Litchfield	Poulton	Worcester
Diss	Liverpool	Romsey	Worcestershire
Doncaster	London	Rowfant (House)	Yarmouth
Dorchester	Louth	Rutland	York
Dorsetshire			Yorkshire

Wales and by the end of 1811 nearly 80 places boasted silver tokens. The following year saw the number of token-issuing communities rise to nearly 100. In some towns more than one trader issued tokens. Chichester, for example, did not have a large population, but seven traders there (including the forerunner of present-day Shippam's) joined in issuing silver tokens.

The sum of £100 would provide 2,000 shillings and an issue of this size was sufficient in many cases to sustain trade in small places.[3] However, in some large towns there were surprisingly large quantities of silver tokens issued. Birmingham, Leeds, Newcastle, Sheffield and York saw their tokens struck over and over again to satisfy the public need. The largest quantity of tokens struck by a single trading group probably was the 600,000 specimens issued jointly by Messrs. Garratt, Terrell, Bird, Beck and Grigg in Bristol. A few of the silver token issuers also issued copper tokens of halfpenny, penny and twopenny denominations; many other traders, however, confined their tokens to the low-value copper issues.

It would be a mistake to assume that such large issues of silver tokens make it easy to find specimens today. In fact, the issuers were usually hard-pressed to redeem the tokens and so promptly melted down all they could get their hands on. At least in one instance the returned tokens were melted down and turned into family plate. The few silver tokens that have survived were held by museums and a handful of collectors who had the foresight to recognize them as chroniclers of the Industrial Revolution.

Given the questionable legal status of the silver tokens, the merchants, bankers and others who dared to issue them took certain precautions to avoid trouble from the government. One technique was to pledge redemption at the rate of twenty shilling tokens per pound.[4] For example, the pledge on the Teignmouth shilling reads: "FOR 20 OF THESE TOKENS WHICH COST ME EACH ONE SHILLING I PROMISE TO PAY THE BEARER A 1 £ BANK OF ENGLAND NOTE I. HOLLAND." Some issuers thought they gained protection against possible government intervention by placing on their tokens the reasons for their issuance. Among the many interesting statements found on shillings are these:

TO FACILITATE TRADE (March, Cambridgeshire), FOR CONVENIENCE OF CHANGE (Barnstaple), FOR PUBLIC ACCOMODATION (Teignmouth), ACCOMMODATION CHANGE (Portsmouth), FOR THE USE OF TRADE (Attleborough), and so on. There were some interesting variations, among them, TO CONVENIENCE THE ARMY AND THE PUBLIC (Ipswich), and optimistic statements such as PROSPERITY TO WALES AND THE CITY OF BRISTOL (Bristol), MAY PLENTY CROWN OUR HAPPY ISLE (Newport, Isle of Wight), and an all-encompassing hope expressed on a Shaftesbury shilling: MAY TRADE THE PLOUGH & THE FLEECE FLOURISH IN ALL THE BRITISH ISLES SUCCESS TO AGRICULTURE AND NAVIGATION.

Statements of Honesty on Silver Tokens

Other issuers were more concerned about the metallic content of their tokens, for it was – after all – the national shortage of silver which brought on the token "revolution" in the first place. J. B. Monck of Reading, who later became a Member of Parliament, did not issue shillings, but his forty shilling gold token and his two silver tokens indicate the actual deadweight content of the metal. The rare Dorchester shillings bear the statement, ONE SHILLING PURE SILVER, while one variety of the Bristol shilling proclaims it to be

PETERBOROUGH CATHEDRAL
This Cathedral is one of only two depicted on silver token shillings (the other: Gloucester). The print at the left is contemporary with the 1811 token.

made from GENUINE DOLLAR SILVER (a reference to the millions of Spanish dollars which had been countermarked with the bust of George III and placed in circulation).

As might be expected, banks were in the forefront as issuers of silver tokens; some also issued bank notes. Guernsey's rare crown piece was issued by the Bank of Guernsey. Other banks and bankers issuing shilling tokens include the Old Bank at Nantwich; the Dorchester (Dorset) Bank; the Old Bank at Marlborough; the Dorset, Wiltshire and Shaftesbury Bank at Shaftesbury; W.S. and I. Wakeford at Andover; Samuel P. Cole at North Lopham (Norfolk); Cole and Company of Peterborough; David Morris and Sons of Carmarthen; and Oakley and Company in Flintshire.

The list of token issuers reads like a directory of business establishments in any town — drapers, grocers, auctioneers, cabinet makers, brewers, tallow chandlers, chemists, ironmongers, silversmiths and goldsmiths, watchmakers, postmasters, jewellers, printers, booksellers, insurance agents, breechesmakers, soap boilers, ropemakers, maltsters, sailcloth makers, wine and spirit merchants, brazier and tinmen, upholsterers, confectioner, bakers, milliners, military tailors and so on. Some of the traders who issued silver tokens were specialists: for example, W. Ballans on his Manchester token describes himself as TEA DEALER MARKET PLACE.

Heraldic Devices Galore

Apart from the array of issuers and the trades they document, the 1811–12 silver tokens are fascinating for the great variety of illustrative devices they employ. By far the most popular

FIVE WELL-KNOWN STRUCTURES ON SILVER TOKENS

From left to right are shilling portraying High Wycombe's Guildhall, the Eddystone Lighthouse (now on Plymouth Hoe), St. Mary's Church in Cheltenham, the Cathedral in Peterborough, and Bristol Bridge as it appeared in 1811.

HERALDRY AND MONUMENTS

Beginning at the left are silver tokens with heraldic devices of Liverpool (an eagle), Leeds (the full arms of the town) and a Lincolnshire type with the suspended fleece enlarged. The fourth token shows Doncaster's Cross of Ote de Tilli, and the last depicts London's statue of Charles I.

A SHIP, A SAINT AND OTHER SUBJECTS

A variety of illustrative devices appears on this group of tokens. From left to right are a sailing ship (Gainsborough), St. Dunstan (Dorchester), a bee skep (Stockport), a ploughman at work (Rowfant, Sussex), and an ancient castle (Scarborough).

is that of the local or county borough arms. Rarely are the arms used in entirety; the central design is usually sufficient to accord the needed association between the token and the town or county of its origin. One of the most artistic of the shilling heraldry series is that issued by the Leeds Workhouse in 1812 portraying the arms of Leeds. Devoid of any lettering or date, the obverse of this splendid coin seemingly has the fleece suspended in space.

Other shillings with heraldic devices include High Wycombe, Nantwich (family arms, the Earls of Cheshire), Cornwall, Launceston, Derby, Barnstaple, Exeter, Teignmouth (Holland family arms), Blandford, Poole, Shaftesbury, Stockton, Gloucester, Hampshire,

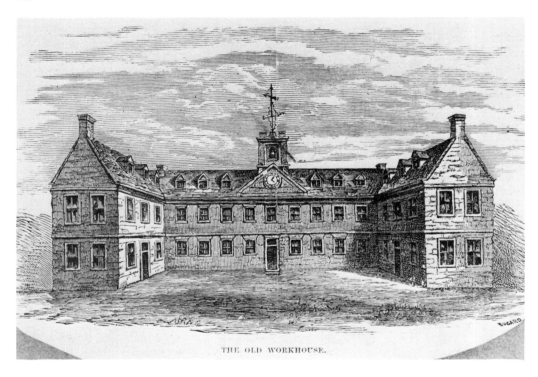

THE OLD WORKHOUSE.

WORKHOUSE AND TOKEN

A well known landmark in Birmingham during the Industrial Revolution was its workhouse. Through its series of silver tokens (the shilling is shown here, enlarged), it became known throughout the land. It was one of two workhouses granted an extension of time for redeeming the coins because of the hardship that would have befallen the poor.

Andover, Portsmouth, Romsey, Southampton, Hereford, the Cinque-Ports, Liverpool, Leicester, Lincoln, London, Bristol, Diss, Bury St. Edmunds, Yarmouth (arms of the Duke of Norfolk), Newcastle, Bath, Stafford, Fazeley (the Harding family), Ipswich, Chichester, Birmingham, Worcester, Bradford, Bridlington, Sheffield, York, Brecknock, Flintshire, Haverfordwest and Jersey.

If this vast range of civic heraldry fails to excite the imagination, there are castles and churches, buildings and busts, cathedrals and crosses, monuments and bridges, and windmills and ships. Ancient battlements, mainly adapted from local arms, adorn the shillings of Barnstaple, Bilston, Chichester, Haverfordwest, Launceston and Neath. Swansea, however, boasts a delightful shilling in two varieties portraying the city's ancient castle.

Two English cathedrals, Gloucester and Peterborough, are featured on shillings of the respective cities, while two churches (both St. Mary's, but in different parts of England) are found on tokens of Cheltenham and Shoreham. The Town Halls of High Wycombe and Newark grace the shillings of these towns, while other buildings are depicted on tokens of Epworth, Stafford and Manchester. One of Britain's largest and most famous workhouses – that at Birmingham – is found on some twenty varieties of the city's shillings.

Busts appear on two of the 1811–14 shillings. The Frome variety purports to portray Edward I, and the second is a likeness of an unknown person on a shilling of Folkestone.

Charles I's Monument on London Tokens

London's famous monument to Charles I, taken down and hidden during the period of the Commonwealth, is the choice for the obverse of six of the capital's shilling tokens. Some portray the statue with lamps on the railings surrounding the monument, some do not. The monument to Otho de Tili adorns a variety of the Doncaster shilling, while down on the Sussex coast the ancient market cross of Chichester is found on some of that city's tokens.

A famous landmark which has changed its appearance over the years, the Bristol Bridge, is featured on two types of Bristol shillings. On the opposite side of the country in Lincolnshire, two Gainsborough shillings show bridges – one ancient, and one contemporary. A token of this town is also the only one in the country to portray a windmill.

Britain's great maritime tradition is reflected on the shillings of several places, all showing graceful sailing ships: Bristol, Gainsborough, Hampshire, Newport, (I.O.W.), Portsmouth, Romsey (hardly a seaport), Southampton, and Bridlington. But perhaps the most appropriate of the maritime devices on shilling tokens is the Eddystone Lighthouse. The famous marker was renowned to seaman the world over, and is also mentioned in a popular sea shanty. The lighthouse portrayed on the tokens is that built by John Smeaton; later – due to water erosion of the rock foundation on which it stood – it had to be replaced. The upper portion of the Smeaton lighthouse stands on Plymouth Hoe today. Several varieties of the Devonshire shilling, as well as one from Exeter and – of all places – Norfolk, feature the Eddystone Lighthouse.

The Banning of the Silver Tokens

The popularity of the tokens, combined with the low intrinsic value of silver in some of them, led some politicians to seek their banning. Up and down the country the public resisted this effort to do away with the useful shillings, sixpences, and other silver tokens. Public meetings were held to defend the "people's coins," but to no avail.[5] Eventually, a series of Acts of Parliament brought an end to the local tokens which had substituted so well for the coin of the realm. By the end of 1814 all had been redeemed and melted down, except for those put aside as keepsakes. Two major issuers, the Birmingham and the Sheffield Workhouses, were given a further period of grace. Each issued large quantities of tokens; these were largely held by the poor, and it was decreed that more time should be

TASMANIAN SHILLING
Australia also had a 19th century silver
token – this attractive shilling issued in
Tasmania and depicting a kangaroo.

given for exchanging these tokens for banknotes or coin of the realm. Thus it is an undeniable fact that the silver tokens of 1811–12 were legal tender because they were not outlawed until Acts of Parliament accorded them extensions of validity, the last of which did not expire until December of 1814.

An Interesting Australian Shilling Token

By way of a postscript to the British silver token series of 1811–12, there was an attractive shilling token issued in Australia a few decades later. Although the coin is dated 1823, local historians believe this refers to the approximate date when the issuer – a sawmill firm, Macintosh and Desgraves – began operations in Tasmania. It seems likely that this silver token was not struck until some years later, perhaps on the occasion of the firm's 25th anniversary.[6]

The obverse of the token depicts a kangaroo, beautifully proportioned, above which appears TASMANIA and below, the date – 1823. The reverse has no illustrative device, but the words ONE SHILLING TOKEN centrally positioned in large letters, while the circular legend reads SAW MILLS MACINTOSH AND DESGRAVES. Very few of the Tasmanian shillings have survived so that only a few of the world's great museums have specimens.

IX
Token Coinage of the Realm

"When the long wars ended, after Waterloo, the currency of the realm was in the most evil condition."

Sir Charles Oman (*The Coinage of England*)

George III was on the throne for 60 years (1760–1820), but only in the last five years of reign did Britons have enough coin of the realm to conduct commerce with ease. This negligence by the government can be put down, in part, to involvement in foreign wars, which had a side effect of making cheap silver bullion difficult to obtain. Indeed, as one historian has pointed out, from 1757 to 1797 it was impossible for the Mint to strike silver coins without incurring a loss on every ounce coined.[1] On those rare occasions when the price of silver did drop slightly, the times were so unstable as to thwart any real effort by the government to remedy the situation.

By 1816, when it was hoped to undertake recoinage, citizens had resorted to just about every substitute imaginable to enable trade to continue. Coin of the realm, when it could be found, was usually worn so thin as to be underweight and illegible. Millions of Spanish dollars had been imported and countermarked, and some French coins also circulated. The private silver tokens, issued mainly in 1811–12, gave some relief, but were outlawed at the end of 1814 – too soon, in the view of some. Finally, as long as speculators could make a profit from the high price of silver, counterfeiting and melting down of coin was bound to continue.

The Great Recoinage of 1816

In May, 1816, the Privy Council Committee on Coin placed its recommendations for a recoinage before the Prince Regent. The Committee knew of the public's willingness to accept coins with less than standard silver content, as demonstrated by the popularity of the 1811–12 silver tokens, and it also was aware of the hectic conditions that attended William III's recoinage. Therefore, it recommended that both the weight and the size of the new shillings (and other silver denominations) be reduced (this would also deter counterfeiting and melting down), and that a sum of £2.5 million in silver be coined before the planned exchange should begin. Finally, it suggested a relatively short period for the exchange.

Three weeks after the proposals were presented, the master of the Mint outlined to employees the measures that would be needed to turn out the desired quantities of coin in the shortest possible time. The master, William Wellesley-Pole, explained that though speed was important, there should be no impairment of the coins' beauty or quality. Minting began in July and continued at a frantic pace for the rest of 1816. New equipment was installed. Additional workers were brought into the Mint from Birmingham. Working hours were extended into the evening, necessitating use of gas light. By mid-August some units of the Mint were working round the clock.

MASSIVE RECOINAGE
Over 23 million shillings dated 1816 and 1817 were issued in 1817 as part of the great recoinage of the Regency period.

With production booming, Pole announced that the exchange of old coins for new would take place in February of 1817. To accomplish this task quickly, over 600 exchange stations were established round the country. Every conceivable type of transport was employed to get the coins to these outlying points – wagons, stage-coaches, caravans – and, in the case of Scotland – ships. After a slight delay in starting, the exchange went off smoothly. When the stations closed a fortnight later on February 27th, the Mint could take satisfaction from a job well done. From the date of placing the Committee's recommendations before the Prince Regent to the closing of the exchange stations, only nine months and one week had elapsed. Not only had the recoinage proceeded with the precision of a classic military operation, but not a single bag or box of coins had gone astray.[2]

By the middle of 1818 almost £4 million in various denominations had been struck. Shillings represented well over half of this total, indicating the coin's relative usefulness. Incidentally, it is a wonder that any of the older coins – especially hammered pieces – survived, given the recoinage efforts of William III and now, that of George III. Shillings dated 1816 onwards are all the same size, and also are legal tender from this date.

The design of the new coins was the most radically altered of any series since the Hanoverians ascended the British throne in 1714. While George III's bust continued to face to the right, this was about the only similarity to his 1787 coins. The new profile shows the influence of another foreign engraver, Benedetto Pistrucci. This brilliant Italian, who was to create the exquisite design of St. George slaying the dragon on sovereigns and crowns of 1817–1820, also prepared a model for the smaller silver denominations. When he came to designing the King's bust, he gave George III a massive head and neck. This design was used in striking the halfcrown and is known as the "bull-head" variety. Happily a slightly modified design, with the size of the neck made smaller, was used on the shilling. Even without the thick neck, however, the royal bust still emphasized the gross features originally created by Pistrucci.

Encircling the profile is the usual royal title with the date of issue placed below. If the massive features of the monarch came as a shock to the viewer in 1817, the coin's reverse – with its decidedly modest aspect – may have offered some consolation. The absurdly long list of titles held by the Hanoverians was gone. In its place was the device of the Order of the Garter inscribed HONI SOIT QUI MAL Y PENSE (Evil to him who evil thinks). Gone, too, was the arrangement of heraldic devices in the form of a cross; the new coin had a shield divided into four quarters. There was one striking difference from previous silver issues: the long-familiar French fleur-de-lys, a feature of English coins since pre-Tudor times, was absent. The reason: Napoleon was unhappy about Britain's continued reference to her monarch being "King of France." By the Treaty of Amiens in 1802, Britain agreed to drop the ancient reference to France; with it also went the fleur-de-lys. Thus, for the first time coin of the realm reflected only elements of the United Kingdom – England, Scotland and Ireland. The arms of Hanover, however, were retained.

Shillings of the new series are dated 1816 to 1820, and there is no change in the design

GEORGE IV AND HIS SHILLING
The King (right) was displeased with the profile on his first coins which included the shilling. An example of the 1821 issue is shown above. Note the arms of Hanover in the centre of the coin's reverse.

except for the dates. Numismatically, the reign of George III had seen great change. There had been a dearth of coins during the first part of his rule, and the last years of his reign had featured token shillings in a prelude to coin of the realm itself becoming "token."

Shillings with the Mintmaster's Initials (WWP)

George IV was fifty-eight when he ascended the throne, and was to reign only ten years. In that short time, however, three distinctive series of shillings were issued in his name. The first was not unlike the last issue of George III. On the reverse, however, were a number of innovations. The central device, a shield bearing the arms of the several parts of the United Kingdom over which the arms of Hanover was imposed, remained much the same as the reverse of George III's last shilling. However, the garter which had encircled the shield was now dropped in favour of a larger crown at the top, a shamrock at the left, a thistle at the right, and a rose at the bottom. It was not considered sufficient to have just the date; the word ANNO was added. Finally, the initials WWP appear in the centre of the leaves on the reverse. These refer to William Wellesley-Pole, the master of the Mint during the recoinage of George III and for a decade afterwards. He came from a gifted family which produced several prominent sons. One brother was Governor-General of India and another was the Duke of Wellington. The mintmaster's initials on the first series of George IV's shillings recall the Tudor period shillings which bear the initials of another famous master, William Sharington. In 1823 the designs of George IV's coins were revised slightly with the principal changes being made on the reverse. The elaborate garnishing was replaced by the simple, but attractive motto of the Order of the Garter. Below the shield again appears the word ANNO and the date – 1823, 1824, and 1825.

Although the first two series of George IV shillings had their busts adapted from the model by Pistrucci, the King was not pleased with his effigy, and ordered the Italian to make a new one based on a bust done by Sir Francis Chantrey. Pistrucci did not like the suggestion that one artist should copy the work of another, and refused. His anger was so great that he worked very little, although he insisted on receiving his salary.

William Wyon, member of a family of master engravers, took over the task of preparing the new bust of the King. It first appears on shillings dated 1825, and continues on others struck in the remainder of the reign. The proportions of the royal effigy are much more flattering than those of the previous coinage. The King must have been satisfied with the Wyon effort, for no further attempt was made at revision. Again, it was the reverse of the shilling which was to reflect the greatest alteration of design. Either the quartered shield, or a cross bearing four armorial devices had dominated the reverse of the shilling since the coin was introduced as a testoon, with only a few exceptions – and those were mainly associated with the period of the Civil Wars and the Commonwealth era. Now both of these were dropped for a new device, the Royal Crest.

The change in the design of the shilling (and sixpence) reverse was for good reason. For generations dishonest people had gilded silver coins and passed them off as gold pieces. Their task was made easier when the silver coins were approximately the same size and weight as the gold pieces they imitated. But when the *appearance* of the silver and gold coins was also similar, the cunning of the rogue was more difficult to thwart. After the accession of George IV, there were complaints that the sixpence was being gilded to look like the half-sovereign. The Mint hastily adopted the Royal Crest reverses for the shilling and sixpence to provide instant distinguishability between silver and gold pieces. Around the crest is a circular legend – spelled out in full for the only time – giving the King's title: BRITAN-NIARUM REX FIDEI DEFENSOR (King of the Britains, Defender of the Faith). The date was shifted from the reverse to the obverse. With this 1825 issue the arms of Hanover disappeared from British coinage.

The reign of George IV was an important one for British coinage for at last the government recognized the need for the denomination most in demand – the shilling – and took effective action. Over 25 million were struck during 1820–29, far more than the number of halfcrowns and sixpences combined.

When George IV died in 1830, there were many who sighed with relief. Many anecdotes and poems were penned to record the passing of "the Georges." Walter Savage Landor, the eminent classicist, spoke for many when he wrote:

> I sing the Georges four
> For Providence could stand no more.
> Some say that far the worst
> Of all was George the First.
> But yet by some 'tis reckoned
> That worse still was George the Second.
> And what mortal ever heard
> Any good of George the Third?
> When George the Fourth from eath descended,
> Thank God the line of Georges ended.

Although the line of Georges may have ended for the time, Britain was to have one more Hanoverian king – William IV. The new monarch was brother of George IV and, at 65, was

WILLIAM IV NAMES THE COIN
The King (left) disliked ostentation, even on his coins. On the reverse of the piece above the Hanoverian arms has been deleted in favour of the value – ONE SHILLING, given for the first time.

the oldest person to ascend the British throne. William was sensitive about the lavish spending and the emphasis on ceremony that had marked much of his brother's reign. His reaction was to adopt, whenever possible, an entirely opposite course. He even opposed his own coronation ceremony, terming it a "useless and ill-timed expense," and insisted on a modest event.

William IV's Shilling: Simple and Straightforward

William Wyon was called upon to design the coinage of William IV, and whether by accident or intention, the shilling reflects the royal dislike of ostentation. Here, except for the Civil War siege pieces, was the simplest design of all – an undecorated bust on the obverse, and a reverse which stated only ONE SHILLING. One interesting feature of William IV's shillings is the employment of GULIELMUS IIII to indicate the King's number in the line of Williams. His brother's coins had the short numbering form, GEORGIUS IV; was William's reversion to the older "IIII" mode another deliberate effort to adopt a style different from that of his brother?

Only occasionally during the shilling's existence was the public able by looking at the coin to make sure that it was a shilling. The Roman numerals XII were included on some early issues, but for the greater part of its "life" up to 1831, the shilling bore nothing to hint at its denomination.

With William IV, however, the uncertainty about the coin's identity was put to an end. The shilling at last had its name stamped on the reverse, even if it had takenen the nation's engravers more than three centuries to do so.

X
Shillings of An Empress and Emperor

"Seeing a piece of money lying on my table, 'I defy', says he, 'any of these active persons to produce half the adventures that this twelve-penny piece has been engaged in, were it possible for him to give us an account of his life'."

Essay (No. 249) from *The Tatler*.

On ascending the throne, Queen Victoria was not permitted to inherit the Hanoverian titles held by successive British kings from George I to William IV.

This exclusion was no affront to the Queen, but merely the result of the operation of the Salic law of succession which governed the Hanoverian dynasty. Under this law a woman could not succeed to the Hanoverian titles. With the accession of Queen Victoria, therefore, Britain was assured of strikingly different shillings from those of the "Four Georges" and William IV. For the first time in more than a century the nation had a woman sovereign, the youngest since the first shillings were struck in the reign of Henry VII.[1]

Victoria was only 18 when she became Queen and few could have foreseen that her reign would extend into the beginning of the twentieth century. This long reign would see many dramatic events in Britain's history, including expansion of the Empire – a fact which the shilling would duly record. Moreover, the Queen's shillings, by the changing royal portrait, would capture the unerring mark of time on the human face.

Probably no other country has been so blessed with engraving talent within a single family as has been Britain with the Wyons. Beginning with Thomas, who bore the principal burden of designing George III's recoinage of 1816, the Mint has seen a procession of Wyons who have left behind some of the most pleasing coin and medal designs of the modern era. Most gifted was William Wyon, who helped his cousin Thomas with the George III designs and remained through the reigns of George IV and William IV. Now, as Queen Victoria came to the throne, he was to achieve his greatest acclaim. Whereas the Italian Benedetto Pistrucci required several sittings of the Queen for his coronation medal (which was to meet with general disapproval), Wyon proved that his workmanship could be as rapid as it was good.

William Wyon's Splendid Profile of the Queen

"William Wyon," recorded Sir John Craig, "made do with one sitting and produced in the young Queen's head one of the finest effigies in English coinage; it was used also for the postage stamps."[2] Although most of his earlier work at the Mint had gone unattributed, his initials – W.W. – now appeared just beneath the Queen's bust on her shillings and other pieces. Queen Victoria's first shillings are dated 1838, although relatively few were struck. Wyon's initials also appeared on some shillings dated 1839, but thereafter they were dropped. The "young head" twelvepenny piece came to be known as the "Elephant Shilling" by three generations of British youth who came across it readily in change. When the face and neck of the Queen are covered by a finger, the bun arrangement of the hair can be

A SHILLING TO ENTER THE GREAT EXHIBITION OF 1851

On certain days the price of admission was reduced to a shilling. The *Punch* cartoon above, entitled "The Pound and the Shilling," depicts an aristocratic family suddenly coming face to face with their servants. The sub-title, "Whoever Thought of Meeting You Here," speaks for itself.

"THE SHILLING DAY GOING TO THE EXHIBITION"

This print shows coachloads of passengers heading for the Great Exhibition in 1851. Fares from many London districts and suburbs were a shilling or less, putting the exhibition within the reach of all. On the first "cheap day" (when the admission was only a shilling), over 18,000 people attended.

THE EXHIBITION TO END ALL EXHIBITIONS

There have been many world fairs, but few can have exceeded the splendid setting of the Crystal Palace, depicted here by J. Tallis. Unlike most fairs, the Great Exhibition of 1851 turned a handsome profit – thanks in part to popular "shilling days".

QUEEN VICTORIA
This shilling is dated 1876 when Queen Victoria became 57. The fine youthful bust of the Queen, executed by William Wyon, was retained on coin of the realm until 1887. The portrait of the Queen (right) was painted in 1883.

imagined to resemble an elephant facing to the right.[3] This initial bust of the Queen was retained on British coinage, with slight modifications, until the Golden Jubilee issue of 1887.

Of the many notable events in the long reign of the Queen one of the most spectacular was the Great Exhibition of 1851. Held in the Crystal Palace and viewed by six million people, it was the brainchild of Prince Albert. However, because he was German-born, the proposal did not at first receive the warm-hearted support for which the Prince hoped. For two years before the event he laboured hard, often at the risk of injuring his health, to perfect the organization of the Exhibition. In the end he carried the day and the Great Exhibition, to this day, has not been equalled in Britain for its splendid setting and range of individual exhibits. The shilling played two minor roles in the Great Exhibition's success. On certain days the admission was reduced to one shilling so that it would be accessible to all. However, the cost of getting to the Exhibition was expensive for the poor and, to overcome this problem, special omnibuses were scheduled for which the fare was only one shilling.

Most national and international exhibitions do well to break even, but the Great Exhibition of 1851 made a profit of nearly £190,000 with which a large acreage in Kensington was bought. On this land there was subsequently erected a group of cultural and scientific centres, among which are the Royal Albert Hall and the Victoria and Albert Museum.

In the middle of Queen Victoria's reign there occurred an unusual development affecting shillings and sixpences. Beginning in 1864 and extending to 1879, tiny die numbers were placed on the reverses of the two denominations just above the dates. The purpose of these was what industrialists call "quality control," and the die numbers may to some degree be

DISAPPOINTING COINAGE
This Golden Jubilee shilling (1887) of
Queen Victoria does not mention the
anniversary, and neither does it state the
coin is a shilling.

compared with the numbered inspection slips that are contained in boxes of chocolates, or
come with new appliances and other manufactured goods.

At the Mint the die number system worked in this way: each coin press in operation
would start off the day with a low-numbered die, attended by an employee whose name was
recorded with the press number and the date. In most cases, a single die number was
probably used for an entire day's output. The following day, the next higher number would
be assigned to dies installed in each press, and so on throughout the year. If a defective
shilling was discovered by a member of the public, the Mint could immediately identify the
"culprit" and his press, as well as the day the inferior coin was made. The inferior pieces
could show signs of a cracked die, of uneven stamping, or the dies simply might be used
beyond the time when they produced faultless coins. Whatever the defect, the tell-tale die
numbers would point to the negligent Mint employee.[4]

Nearly 900 Die Varieties on Queen Victoria's Shillings

Die No. 1 appears on shillings of Queen Victoria for each year between 1864 and 1879,
when the numbering system was abolished. However, the numbers employed annually
varied greatly; only 15 numbers were used in 1869, but at least 131 appeared on dies in
1872. An average of about 56 different numbers was employed annually during the period
when the system operated. Queen Victoria shillings still turn up with hitherto unreported
die numbers. By 1979 the total had reached 895, but the final figure may well go beyond
900.

Producing large amounts of quality coins was not a concern peculiar to Queen Victoria's
moneyers. In Tudor times, when all coins were hammered, the problem was just as acute.
Considering the crudeness of the hammered system and the uneven blows struck by the
human hand, it is amazing that up to 20,000 coins could be produced from the same set of
dies. When the first milled coins were made in Britain, some of the machines were found to
exert so much pressure that dies lasted for no more than 1,000 coins. Eventually the presses
were improved and the figure per die set was brought back to, and sometimes surpassed,
that of the Tudor period. In the reign of George III the newly-developed lever press made it
possible to strike as many as 50,000 coins from the same dies. By the end of Queen
Victoria's reign as many as 130,000 shillings could be struck from the same set of dies.

In the 1850s a concentrated effort was made by Britain's business community to
persuade the country to adopt decimal coinage. Despite a nationwide publicity campaign,
this effort failed. One reason for public skepticism was a fear of hidden inflation. Many
people believed, for example, that a decimalized shilling would allow them to buy only ten
articles (such as a penny postage stamp) instead of the customary dozen.

As Queen Victoria approached the Golden Jubilee year of her reign in 1887 the public
eagerly awaited the striking of special coins to mark the occasion. In every village, town and

THE QUEEN'S LAST SHILLING

The design of Queen Victoria's third shilling, showing the monarch veiled, was unchanged for the last nine years of her life.

city commemorative events were planned, some of them elaborate, and it was assumed that a series of coins especially designed to mark the anniversary would be forthcoming. Moreover, the British Empire had expanded greatly during the Queen's reign and national pride had seldom been greater. At the very least, the public expected one or more coins inscribed with the Jubilee dates, 1837–1887.[5]

Great was the dismay, therefore, when details of the Jubilee coinage became known. True, the Queen's bust would be altered from a youthful to an older one, but not a word would appear about the Golden Jubilee and neither would the anniversary dates be given. Aside from the new profile, now more in keeping with the Queen's age, the other feature which distinguished the coins from previous ones was a ridiculously small crown perched – precariously it seemed – upon the Queen's head. The public, appalled at what they saw, universally condemned the coins as being inadequate for so momentous an occasion. One noted historian, Sir Charles Oman, described the Jubilee issue as "the greatest disappointment of the century."[6]

The Shilling with No Mark of Denomination

A closer examination of Queen Victoria's Jubilee shilling revealed other disappointments. The bust was disproportionately small for the size of the coin. The shoulders of the Queen were too ornate. More disconcerting was something which hung from the Queen's head; this was supposed to have been a veil, but it looked more like a long strand of hair, or some odd material dangling loosely. It was the lack of a denominational value on the shilling (and other coins) that probably annoyed most people. Over 90 million Jubilee silver coins were struck between 1888 and 1892 – among them 30 million shillings – but none indicated its value. It was as if Britain had slipped back into the era of hammered coins.

So great was the outcry against the unpopular coins that two years later a modified version appeared. The revised design presents a more pleasing bust, one which is both larger and more tastefully executed. A larger crown now adorns Victoria's head and a flowing veil falls gracefully over her shoulders. There is little change on the reverse.

Even with these modifications the issue was an artistic failure; in 1891 a committee was set up to recommend a new design. A competition was held after which the effigy of the Queen executed by Thomas Brock was selected as the model for the next (and final) coinage of Victoria. This bust displayed markedly aged features, and coins bearing it were promptly called the "old head" series. The 1893 shilling is unchanged except that the royal title for the first time refers to the sovereign's status on the world scene – INDIAE IMPERATRIX (Empress of India). The Queen actually became Empress in 1876, but the thought of including the Indian title seems to have eluded the coin designers for seventeen years. The IND. IMP. reference was to remain part of the royal title right up to the 1948 shilling of George VI. Even if it was more than a decade late in doing so, the shilling had chronicled the rise of the British Empire.

EDWARD VII: ONE TYPE
The King (left) reigned nine years
and only one type of shilling (shown
above) was issued during this brief
period.

The reverse of Queen Victoria's final shillings has a trefoil made up of the heraldic devices of England, Scotland and Ireland, with the value, ONE SHILLING, at the top, and the date below. The first shilling of Victoria is dated 1838, the last 1901; thus to form a complete collection of shillings of this reign is a formidable task. If one includes die varieties, the figure is over 900 – the largest number for any British monarch.

When Queen Victoria died in January of 1901, she had reigned longer (63 years) and lived to a greater age (81 years and nearly eight months) than any other British sovereign.

The Queen's eldest son, Edward was 59 at his mother's death, and already a grandfather. Although destined to live only nine more years – a period so brief it allowed no real variation in his coinage – Edward did make a considerable impact on Britain's foreign relations and upon the domestic social scene.

Like the Hanoverian monarchs before her, Queen Victoria distrusted her heir's abilities and involved him only minimally in national affairs. Thus deprived of a role at home, he spent much time travelling abroad where his fluency in languages and charm made him popular with European leaders. In particular, he worked hard to improve Britain's relations with France, for the centuries-old enmity between the two nations still lurked just below the surface. Fortunately, these efforts to bring the two countries closer together were to prove of great benefit during the First World War. The King was also to set the style in fashion and his love of sport endeared him to many like-minded citizens.

"King of All the Britains"

The exquisite profile of Edward VII which appears on his shillings was executed by G. W. de Saulles. The King's features are brilliantly captured in a bust facing to the right. In the legend of this shilling a new element appears: instead of referring to the royal title, King of Britain, the legend now reads BRITT. OMN. REX (King of All the Britains). This reference was designed to remind subjects residing in far-flung corners of the Empire that their homelands were considered as other "Britains" lying beyond the British Isles.

Although Edward's shillings were issued each year from 1902 to 1910, only those struck in 1902, 1906, and 1910 were produced in large quantities. Those dated 1905 numbered less than 500,000 and, as many of these became badly worn or were melted down, this issue is by far the rarest in the King's series of shillings.

When Edward VII died in 1910 the royal family took the unusual step of authorizing an official photograph. Although this much-published picture was made nine years after the King's first shillings were struck, his photographic profile bears a striking resemblance to the portrait executed by de Saulles on the coins.

XI
Farewell to the British Shilling

"I have touched the highest point of my greatness;
And from that full meridian of my glory,
I haste now to my setting . . . ."

Wolsey in "King Henry VIII" (Act III).

George V's shillings proclaimed him Emperor of India and one of his first decisions after ascending the throne was to plan a state visit to the Indian sub-continent. As Prince of Wales he had visited India earlier; that visit left him convinced that Britain should never cease its efforts to maintain close and friendly relations with the people of India.

In early November of 1911 the King sailed from Portsmouth in H.M.S. *Medina* and three weeks later arrived in Bombay. After a few days in the port city, the royal party moved on to Delhi where a massive durbar (public levee) had been planned. The Delhi Durbar was a coronation one and some of the King's advisors were concerned about security risk, but the King dismissed these fears and enthusiastically entered into the occasion. The durbar was an overwhelming success. Some 300,000 people attended, a considerable portion of whom were housed in a "city" of 40,000 tents. The manifestations of loyalty were many, and the King was deeply moved. Later he said the durbar had surpassed all expectations and the visit to India, he added, had been fully worth the effort and the long journey.

For a century and a half Britain's monarchs had been either Hanoverian or from Saxe-Coburg-Gotha. George V, no doubt influenced by the major event of his reign – the First World War, decided the time had come to drop the Germanic associations with the British monarchy. Thus, although he ascended the throne as a member of the House of Saxe-Coburg-Gotha, he became the first British sovereign of the House of Windsor after the dynasty's name was changed.

Except for the inclusion of the initials of the designer of the King's bust, Sir Bertram MacKennal, on the truncation beneath the profile, there was no major change in the design of George V's shillings from those of Edward VII. The King's title still designated him as ruler of "all the Britains" and his first shillings continued to be struck in the old standard of .925 silver.

Another Debasement of the Coinage

In 1920 there occurred another of those periods when the price of silver rose so high that the government could no longer issue silver coinage of the same size and standard (.925) without incurring a loss. There were several choices: doing nothing (as happened during most of George III's reign), reducing the size of the shilling and other coins (as with the 1816 issue), or debasing the coinage by using more alloy. The third course was adopted, and the 1920 issue appeared with a 50–50 proportion of silver and alloy, the first time in more than three centuries that English coinage had been debased.

For the next seven years the Mint experimented with various dies and combinations of metals. The inevitable result was that some coins had reliefs that eroded quickly. Shillings

GEORGE V: EMPEROR
The King (left) is shown in Delhi at the time of the durbar of 1911. For the occasion a special crown (above) was made in India. George V was the first reigning British monarch to visit India.

dated 1920 to 1926 that circulated normally are seldom found with anything more than the date and legend recognizable.

A "modified effigy" shilling appeared in 1926 with the royal bust slightly reduced in size and with other small alterations to the previous design. The following year saw a change in the coin's reverse. The inner circle immediately surrounding the lion and crown was dropped; this permitted an enlargement of the central design. No alteration was made in the legend of the reverse, but the initials of the engraver, Kruger Gray, appeared at the tip of the lion's tail.

King George V's reign saw many crises and confrontations, including the First World War, upheaval in Ireland and the General Strike of 1926. The troubles in Ireland led to the Government of Ireland Act of 1920 and subsequently to independent coinage for "Saorstat Eireann" (1928) and for Eire in 1939.

For the last decade of George V's reign there were no changes in his shillings and other coins. The last of these were dated 1936, but virtually all were struck after the King's death (January, 1936) when Edward VIII was on the throne.

The Shillingless Reign

With the exception of Lady Jane Grey's "reign" of only nine days, the reign of Edward VIII was to be the shortest of any monarch since the shilling was instituted in the time of Henry

GEORGE V: DEBASED COINAGE

The reign of George V saw another debasement of Britain's coinage, this time to a standard of 50% silver and 50% alloy. The 1920 shilling (left) was the first in the series to be struck in the debased metal.

A DIFFERENT REVERSE

A modified shilling design (right) was used for the last 11 years of George V's reign. An enlarged lion and crown on the reverse were the most obvious changes.

VII. It endured less than a year and came to an end not because he was incompetent or unpopular, but rather because of his decision to abdicate and marry a divorcee. Thus the country was spared a crisis that would have involved both constitutional and religious issues.

Edward ascended the throne 20 days after the start of 1936 and quitted it 20 days before the year's end, but not without providing the nation and the world a dramatic ending – sudden abdication. Unknown to the general public, there was going on at the same time a parallel drama concerning Edward VIII's coinage where the King also let his personal views be known.

To appreciate the almost unprecedented interest in coin of the realm displayed by the King, it is necessary to review the steps leading to the issue of coins depicting a new monarch. The process takes many months and sometimes a year or longer, for first artists must submit proposed designs and then a committee (or committees) must examine them in detail. The designs obviously must conform to high standards of dignity and artistry, the legend must be carefully scrutinized to see that there is nothing offensive to the nation as a whole or its constituent parts, and – perhaps most important of all – the royal image must be pleasing. Although the various steps involved took time, the moneyers at the Royal Mint nonetheless had every hope of placing Edward VIII's coins into circulation early in 1937.

When the experts narrowed down the designs and were assured that the legends were suitable, the time came for obtaining the royal assent. The King took a keen interest in the proposed coinage, but objected to two aspects in particular: the direction in which his profile should face, and the continued use of existing devices on the reverse of the coins.[1]

Traditionally the direction in which the royal busts face alternate with successive reigns. Since that of George V had faced left, that of Edward ought to have faced to the right. When the King was shown a wax model of a right-facing profile, the Deputy Master of the Royal Mint hoped the sovereign would agree to retaining the alternating arrangement. But, as a report later revealed, "... this ... the King did not like, his misgivings arising from a firm conviction that the features of the left side of his face were superior to those of the right."[2] Put plainly, the parting of the King's hair showed up on a left-facing profile, but not on a right-facing one.

EDWARD VIII: FEW SHILLINGS
Had Edward VIII (right) remained King only a few weeks more, his coins would have been struck. The shilling above is one of very few pattern pieces that have survived.

The King Chooses His Profile

Great was the dilemma of the Deputy Master of the Mint. ". . . the King had a perfect right to appear on his coins in the way he wished and the argument was reinforced by . . . [the lack of] any practical reason to justify alternating effigies," continued the report of the problem. "Yet . . . numismatic traditions are not lightly to be broken," it stated, "especially those relating to the dignity of the Crown, and the Deputy Master was fully conscious of the public controversy that would ensue were the King's wishes to be followed."[3] In the end the King's wishes prevailed and a "parted-hair" profile, facing left, was adopted for the proposed coinage.

With the obverse design thus settled, there remained the matter of deciding upon the reverse. Although a new monarch's accession always provided an opportunity to change the reverse designs of coins, in fact little alteration was usually made and it was the view of the Royal Mint's Advisory Committee that not much modification was needed on the forthcoming issue of Edward VIII's coins. When the subject of the reverse designs was broached in an audience with the Deputy Master of the Mint, it was apparent for the first time that the King had definite ideas on the subject. "While not disliking the existing designs," the Mint report said, ". . . [the King] seemed inclined to think that he should have his own set of coins, and showing the Deputy Master some foreign coins on his watch chain, asked if a more modern coinage could be designed."[4]

The Deputy Master was thrown into despair, for a radical change of the reverse of the coin of the realm had not been contemplated. For one thing, what did the King mean by "modern?" For another, where could artists be found quickly to create modern designs –

whatever they were? And, finally, what of the problem of getting agreement on such designs and the inevitable delay it would involve? Then followed a period of considering one category or another of subjects for the coins' reverses – buildings, factories, aircraft, marine life and animals. "Not surprisingly," the Mint report continues, "the suggestion of subjects proved to be a task which no one seemed particularly anxious to undertake . . . ."[5] A zoological set of designs, among which the reverse of the shilling bears a sturgeon, was shown the King in July of 1936. But on this occasion the King backed down from his previously expressed wish for "modern" designs, and agreed that the British public might not take kindly to the zoological reverses.

The "Scottish Reverse" Is Born

Meanwhile, Mr. Kruger Gray had been quietly working on new reverse designs, among them a shilling which incorporated the Scottish crest. Scots had long felt their nation had been left out of designs on the kingdom's coinage; now, with the coin reverses undergoing change, here was the chance to include a distinctively Scottish reverse. Mr. Gray, implementing the request of the Deputy Master to prepare a Scottish reverse for the Edward VIII shilling, conceived the design which was subsequently employed on George VI's "Scottish" shillings. Patterns bearing these new reverses were almost ready for the royal approval when the King's abdication was announced.

Very few sets of the pattern pieces survived the long and frustrating effort to design the new coinage for Edward VIII. Of these, one is in the Queen's collection, one is held by the Royal Mint, and at least one is owned by a private collector. Since the King's abdication, six Edward VIII coins were advertised for sale by a London coin dealer.[6] In the prospectus the coins (the farthing up to the crown) were priced at £250,000 and billed as "the rarest and most expensive set of coins in the world;" the shilling was listed at £25,000.

Had the King's abdication been delayed by a few weeks, Britain might have had its Edward VIII coins. However, four overseas areas did receive and circulate coins of Edward VIII – British West Africa, British East Africa, New Guinea and Fiji. None are scarce, for their combined mintage exceeded 78 million pieces; the smallest quantity struck was the Fiji penny (120,000). None were shillings.

George VI: A Valiant Monarch

As Duke of York, George VI had little expectation of becoming King. Moreover he was not a robust man. Yet he courageously accepted the responsibility which fell to him after his brother's abdication. He was to be plagued by ill health and die at the early age of 56, but not before gaining the wholehearted admiration of his subjects in the Second World War – a conflict that was to endure for nearly half his reign.

Although the Second World War was to affect the King's shillings drastically, George VI's first shillings, dated 1937, were commonplace except for being issued with separate reverses for England and Scotland. The obverses were identical, bearing the royal profile and the customary legend. The reverse of the "English shilling" is only slightly modified from that on the shillings of George V – the *statant regardant* lion of England astride the crown. The "Scottish shillings," as mentioned earlier, had been designed for Edward VIII's shillings until the abdication put an end to striking the coinage. The attractive Scottish shilling has for its reverse the lion of Scotlant seated on the crown with a sword in one paw

GEORGE VI: WAR-TIME KING

The King (right) saw the transition of the British Empire to the Commonwealth of Nations. His shillings (below) recorded India's emergence as an independent nation. Despite fragile health, the King insisted on visiting troops abroad and sites of enemy bombing at home.

ENGLISH–SCOTTISH

At the left and right are the English and Scottish shilling reverses with (centre) an identical obverse. Below are the same reverses after omission of IND:IMP.

and a sceptre in the other. Unlike the English counterpart, the Scottish shilling's reverse contains two small shields, one containing a thistle and the other the Cross of St. Andrew.

With the end of the Second World War came two significant developments in British coinage. In 1947 appeared the first shillings with no silver at all. The so-called silver shillings dated 1920 to 1946 had in fact contained only 50% silver, but continuing even this standard was no longer possible at a time when Britain had to repay the United States for 88 million ounces of silver borrowed during the war. The new pieces, composed of an alloy of 75% copper and 25% nickel, provided a hard-wearing surface whose appearance was not unlike that of silver. Following the Second World War many other countries also abandoned silver coinage. For Britain the era of silver change was over, and only proof pieces, Maundy coins, and some commemorative pieces would hereafter be struck in silver. The other coin alteration deriving from the war was the dropping of that part of the royal title referring to the King as Emperor of India. The IND. IMP. which had been on shillings since 1893, was no longer appropriate with India's status as an independent nation and was omitted on coins from 1949 onwards.

SECOND WORLD WAR AFFECTS THE CONTENT OF COINS
In this photograph a convoy of ships from the United States is approaching Britain
with essential supplies and armaments. Among the commodities borrowed from the
United States was a large quantity of silver. To repay this loan in kind, the government obtained silver by melting down some coin in circulation. Starting in 1947,
coin of the realm contained no silver.

Britain's Last Shillings

Queen Elizabeth II became the sixth woman to reign over Britain since the shilling was first
struck under Henry VII. By 1966, when the country's last shillings were issued, Britain had
been ruled longer by women than by men since the reign of George III. With the exception
of Queen Victoria, she was the nation's youngest woman to be crowned since Elizabeth I.

With the accession of the Queen to the throne the Royal Mint once more was faced with
the task of producing new coinage. Obviously the obverse now must carry the Queen's
profile, but would there also be changes on the reverse? Any change in the wording of the
legends on either side seemed unnecessary, but here was an opportunity to alter or improve
the reverse designs. While adhering to the precedent on the reverses of her father's shillings
on which English and Scottish designs were used, the Mint now decided to drop the large,
perhaps disproportionate lions, and replace them with heraldic devices of the same size.
The English shield has three lions, that of Scotland a rampant lion, and both are crowned.

However, it was the Queen's profile which was to be the main preoccupation of the Royal
Mint's Advisory Committee. As usual, the first step was to issue invitations for profile

QUEEN ELIZABETH II: TROOPING OF THE COLOUR
When the first shilling appeared, England expected her kings to lead troops into battle. This tradition continued until 1743 when George II, at Dettingen, became the last reigning monarch to do so. In the more peaceful reign of Queen Elizabeth II, when the last shilling was struck, the demands upon the sovereign for public and ceremonial appearances greatly increased. In the photograph above the Queen leads the Brigade of Guards back to Buckingham Palace after the Trooping ceremony.

BRITAIN'S LAST SHILLINGS
With the reign of Queen Elizabeth II, the shilling bowed out as an official denomination. Her shillings continued the custom of English and Scottish reverses begun in the time of her father, George VI; the English type is shown above at the right, and the Scottish variety below. In 1954 the words BRITT. OMN. (ruler of all the Britains) were omitted (compare the obverses).

designs; then came the task of evaluating them. In this scrutiny the committee was fortunate in having as its president, Prince Phillip. Eventually it was agreed that the profile to be employed should be the delicately designed one submitted by Mary Gillick.

In 1954 there was a small, but important change in the Queen's title as reflected on her shillings and other coins. Since the first coinage of Edward VII in 1902 shillings, and other denominations, had borne the words BRITT. OMN. – (ruler of) "all the Britains" (i.e., including overseas areas). As the British Empire had long since given way to a grouping of independent countries known as the British Commonwealth of Nations, the term BRITT. OMN. was obsolete. It had been used on the Queen's first coins dated 1953; with its omission thereafter, no further changes took place on her shillings.

The double issue of English and Scottish varieties of the Queen's shillings dated 1966 were the last pieces of the denomination to be struck as coin of the realm. A souvenir issue dated 1970 (not for general circulation) appeared after the shilling's successor – the five penny piece – was introduced (1968). It was decimal coinage, officially inaugurated on 15 February 1971, that dealt the death blow to the shilling. The proposal that Britain should adopt decimal coinage came as early as the reign of Charles II and, as has been related earlier, was given serious attention in government reports in 1859 and 1920. As one of the great trading nations of a world already dedicated to the principle of decimal coinage, Britain was obliged to adopt a system (retaining the pound as the basic unit) in which silver coins would lose their old names and instead become so many pence – 5, 10 and so on – each easily divided into 100.

Thus in the reign of Queen Elizabeth II the shilling, which by its ever-changing designs, royal profiles and legends had recorded so much of British history, came to an end as an official denomination of the coin of the realm.

XII
Anglo-Irish and Scottish Shillings

". . . such of our subjects within this kingdom, as shall refuse to receive the . . . pieces of copper and brass money . . . being tendered to them for payment shall be punished according to the utmost vigour of the law, as contemners of our royal prerogative and commands."
Extract from one of the several proclamations on gun-money by James II.

Although the story of the shilling is essentially an English or a British one, there were separate issues of shillings in Ireland during the Tudor and Stuart reigns, and to a lesser degree, Scottish shillings during the Stuart dynasty. Modern Irish shillings are grouped with those of other nations in the following chapter.

The early Irish shillings fall into two distinctive groups.[1] The first were struck as part of the normal Anglo-Irish coinage during the Tudor period and the beginning of the Stuart dynasty. The second group appeared during the reign of Charles I, embracing the Civil War pieces, and the reign of James II, comprising the famous "gun-money" shillings and other denominations. While the first category comprised coins circulated under perfectly normal circumstances, those that appeared in the reigns of Charles I and James II were all emergency issues reflecting the chaos of the period.

The First Anglo-Irish Shilling

The English testoon was issued in the reigns of Henry VII and Henry VIII, but it was not until Edward VI ascended the throne that a shilling appeared with a distinctive mintmark for Ireland. This issue, a base one, was dated MDLII (1552) and bears the Irish harp mintmark; otherwise, it is similar to the Edward VI base issue of England. It is extremely rare, but contemporary brass imitations of this coin are also known.

The Irish gave this base shilling of Edward VI a subtle nickname when the coin was later cried down to a third of its face value. They were called "bungals" by the populace, an appellation derived from the Irish *bunn geal* (white groat). The term became so widely accepted in Ireland that it later came to be applied to all the coinage of inferior standard produced during the Tudor dynasty.

Mary Tudor's Only Shilling with Her Portrait Alone

It was not until Mary Tudor became Queen that there was a truly Irish shilling. This piece, struck only for the first two years of Mary's reign and before her marriage to Philip of Spain, is the only shilling which bears the Queen's profile without that of her husband. The obverse portrays a crowned Mary facing left, and the legend reads MARIA: D:G ANG: FRA: Z HIB: REGINA. There are varieties with minor differences in the spelling or abbreviation. The reverse presents a crowned harp flanked by the initials M and R, each of which is also crowned. Its legend has the date, 1553 or 1554, in Roman numerals and the motto VERITAS TEMPORIS FILIA (Truth, the daughter of Time). Happily, Mary's

MARY'S SHILLING
The Irish shilling (right) of Mary I is the only one depicting her without her husband, Philip.

PHILIP AND MARY
This shilling of Philip and Mary (left) is similar to the English type, except for the harp reverse.

shillings were struck with more than 50% silver content, for when the Queen's next shilling appeared – depicting her with her husband, an era of a more debased coinage began which was to last well into the reign of Elizabeth I.

The Philip and Mary shilling is similar to its English counterpart, having the same arrangement of facing busts with the crown above. The same legend is used with a slight difference in abbreviation. All the Anglo-Irish Philip and Mary shillings bear the date 1555 just below the royal portraits. The coin is considered to be a billon one; that is, more than half its content is copper. Its reverse has the same basic design found on the shilling of Mary, except that the legend reads POSUIMUS DEUM ADIUTOREM NOSTRUM (We have made God our Helper) and the initials P and M are substituted for the letters M and R.

Three issues of shillings were struck in Ireland during the reign of Elizabeth I. The first two have busts of the Queen on the obverse, portraying her in the attractive ruffs of the Tudor period. The reverse of this first issue has a central device of the Irish harp flanked by the crowned initials, E and R. With the next issue, the reverse drops the large harp in favour of three smaller ones arranged in a triangular pattern on an escutcheon or shield, and flanked by two digits of the dates, 15 appearing at the left, and 61 on the right. The third issue, struck during the last three years of Elizabeth's reign, is unique in that it is the only one from the queen's reign which does not bear her portrait. A shield of the Royal arms, similar to that found on the reverse of some of her English coins, now graces the obverse of this Anglo-Irish shilling; the reverse has a large harp, crowned.

Legends on Elizabeth's Anglo-Irish shillings are similar to those on her English coins. The old religious motto, POSUI DEUM ADIUTORE MEUM, remains a favourite. The metallic content of Elizabeth's shillings varies greatly. That in her second issue shillings has an unusually high silver content (roughly 11/12ths), but that in the other two issues is comprised of billon alloy of which silver constitutes only about twenty-five per cent.

Ireland's last regular issue of shillings came in the reign of James I. This time the shilling

ELIZABETH'S COIN
The Irish harp is a distinctive feature of the Elizabeth I shilling shown at the left.

JAMES' SHILLING
This shilling of James I (right) was the last in the series of regular coinage struck for Ireland.

contained 9 ounces of fine silver to 3 of alloy and, since the coins were also struck in the London mint, the obverses are similar to the English shillings of James I – although the reverses bear crowned harps. The familiar EXURGAT DEUS, etc., legend appears on James' first Anglo-Irish shillings (1603–4); his second issue pieces (1604–7) bear the famous "proclamation" documenting the King's unification of England, Scotland and Ireland: HENRICUS ROSAS REGNA JACOBUS (Henry united the roses, James the Kingdoms).

Irish Emergency Shillings

History records many instances when subject peoples, feeling themselves oppressed, rise up against their rulers when their masters are busy with domestic troubles. Such was the case in 1642 when the Catholics in Ireland, finding much of their land occupied by English settlers and facing the prospect of a Puritan Parliament, decided the moment had come to rebel. However, there were both English Catholics and Irish Catholics living in Ireland and their interests did not always coincide. The English Catholics supported Charles I, but did not wish their religious freedom jeopardized. Irish Catholics, on the other hand, were unwilling to accept Charles because he represented England.

The picture was further complicated by the formation of small, but well organized Protestant movements in Ireland – the settled Anglo-Irish of the Pale, and the Planters with Scottish Covenanter troops mainly in the North. Given such fragmentation of effort and the scattered nature of the fighting, it was inevitable that some forces would be hemmed in and left to their own resources for survival. Thus emerged the Irish siege pieces of the rebellion, a coinage which included three basic types of shillings.

The Inchiquin Money

First of these shillings of necessity was a piece of the so-called "Inchiquin" money, struck in 1642. A crudely cut portion of silver plate, this shilling may have been intended more as a

INCHIQUIN PIECE

Issued by the Lord Justices of Ireland, this shilling (right) was one of several denominations struck in 1642. It bears the same stamp on both sides: 3:21 (for 3 pennyweight, 21 grains). Strictly speaking, these pieces were tokens.

ORMONDE MONEY

Struck in 1643 on a crude flan, this shilling (left) bears the crown and initials, CR, on its obverse, and the value, XII D, on the reverse. Seven denominations were issued, ranging from twopence to a crown.

token than a coin. Although having neither date nor issuing authority, it bears in a beaded circle the actual weight of silver it contains: dwt: gr 3:21. This weight is stamped on both sides, and there is no other illustrative device on this unusual piece. Besides the shilling, the series includes crowns, halfcrowns, ninepences, sixpences, groats and threepences – each denomination bearing its respective weight. As the Dublin moneyers had no equipment for producing rounded flans, the Inchiquin pieces are irregularly shaped. At first it was thought these siege pieces were issued by authority of the Vice President of Munster, Lord Inchiquin (hence their name), but it is now generally believed that the coins were struck under the auspices of Ireland's Lords Justice.

The second series of Irish siege pieces is known as "Ormonde" money, but as with the earlier pieces, this attribution is now in doubt. The Marquis of Ormonde (later Lord Lieutenant of Ireland) was a strong supporter of Charles I and led the Royalist forces against the opposition. Whether these pieces deserve to be attributed to Ormonde is perhaps academic, for his name is by now firmly identified with them, and there is documentary evidence that he issued two gold denominations (pistole and double pistole) in 1646.

Again, there were several denominations, less irregularly shaped this time, and among them was a shilling. On these pieces the King's association is not left in doubt; the obverse features the initials CR beneath the crown, while the reverse shows the value X.II below the letter D. There is no date, but these pieces are believed to have been issued around 1643.

The final series of Irish siege pieces, like their English counterparts, are associated with specific localities. On the south coast of Ireland were four towns – at no great distance apart – which were caught up in the bitter fighting: Youghal, Cork, Kinsale, and Bandon. Their garrisons took a determined stand against the Catholics and, thus beleaguered, were obliged to strike their own coins.

These pieces were mostly minor denominations, but at Cork a shilling was also issued.

THE CORK SHILLING OF 1647

Cork was one of four Munster towns known as "Cities of Refuge" held by Parliamentary troops. Cork was the only one to issue a shilling; it also issued halfpennies and sixpences.

Cut roughly octagonal, it bears the town's name, CORK, and the date, 1647, on the obverse, and the value, XII, on the reverse. The Confederate Catholics, centred on Kilkenny, struck their own series of coins, but the shilling is unknown.

Thus, the period of the Irish Rebellion is documented by the shillings of the Lords Justice and Ormonde, and a "local money" series. Just as the memorable events of the English Civil Wars were being recorded numismatically by the siege coins of Carlisle, Newark, Pontefract and Scarborough, so were the moneyers of Ireland busily engaged in striking their own emergency pieces. On both sides of the irish Sea these coins of necessity were to become vivid and lasting reminders of troubled times and the foremost denomination among them was the shilling.

Shillings from Old Guns, Pots and Pans

If one were to seek a numismatic memento of the troubles in Ireland, none would be more appropriate than one of the "gun-money" shillings of James II.

After leaving England, the King fled to France where he attempted to muster enough support to try and regain the throne by way of Ireland. With a contingent of French troops and supporting weapons and supplies, he landed at Kinsale on March, 1688. Soon Ireland was plunged into bloodshed and there followed a rough division of the population into Irish (mainly Catholic) and British (mainly Protestant) camps. The resulting animosity was so great that its effects have endured to this century.

To be reliable, any army must have good morale and the key ingredients of this are ample provisions and regular, adequate pay. James was made painfully aware of this truth when he became hard-pressed to finance his military operations in Ireland. His first step was to increase the value of English coin in circulation by $8\frac{1}{2}\%$ (gold was raised by 20%). French $3\frac{1}{2}$ sou pieces, brought over with the French troops, were ordered to pass for double their face value. However, none of these measures was sufficient to maintain James' forces and allow normal trading. More coins were needed urgently

"We Have Ordered . . . Copper and Brass Money"

In mid-1689 he established two mints, one at Dublin and the other at Limerick. Simultaneously he instructed his agents to lay their hands upon brass and all other metals suited to coinage. He then issued a series of royal proclamations, one of which dealt with shillings. The first part explained why the emergency coin issue was necessary: "Whereas, for remedy of the present scarcity of money in this our kingdom, and [so] that our standing forces may be the better paid and subsisted, and that our subjects of this realm may be the better enabled to pay and discharge the taxes, excises, customs, rents, and other debts and

THE DUBLIN MINT OF JAMES
Here most of the King's gun-money was coined. The house, at 27 Capel Street, is reputed to be the birthplace of Thomas Sheridan, the actor.

duties which are or shall be hereafter payable to us, we have ordered a certain quantity of copper and brass money to be coyned and pass as currant in this our kingdom during our pleasure . . . ." This justification for striking coins in base metals was common to all the royal proclamations, but a provision for each denomination was precisely stated. ". . . each piece of the . . . twelve penny pieces," it read, ". . . [must have] on one side the effigies or figure of our head with this inscription round, JACOBUS II DEI GRATIA, and upon the other side the stamp or impression of cross-sceptres and a crown between J.R. with XII above, the month wherein they are coyned below with this inscription round, MAG.BRIT. FRAN. & HIBER. REX. 1689, and fringed round . . ."[2]

The coinage proclamations of James II are remarkable documents. First, they freely admit to the need for emergency coins. They also make it clear that money was needed primarily for supporting the army, with consideration for the general public coming second. Then, perhaps to discourage counterfeiting, they stated precisely the design and wording of each denomination. If some were in doubt about the intrinsic value of the base coins, the royal proclamation reminded them punishment awaited any who refused to accept the gun-money pieces. Another unusual aspect of the proclamations was the requirement that the coins bear the month, as well as the year of issue.

"The material from which these gun-money coins were struck was largely composed of old church bells, kitchen utensils and disused cannon, hence the name," writes one scholar. "They were now, however, to become more harmful to friend than to foe, and they forcefully recall to mind the conversion of swords into ploughshares. Gun-metal was at this period (1689–90) worth from three pence to four pence per pound, but now, by the necessities of the time, was forced into circulation at a greatly enhanced value."[3]

Coins of Base Metal, but Well Designed

If the metal content of James II's coinage in Ireland left much to be desired, the same could not be said for the workmanship of the shilling and other pieces. It was an excellent standard, thanks to the effort of the faithful Stuart engraver, Jan Roettier. The bust of James is clear and detailed, and the remainder of the design – however intricate, is artistically executed.

Scraping together the brass and copper required for the Irish coinage turned out to be an onerous task, even with the full weight of royal authority behind such efforts. Fortunately, a number of documents survive to illustrate these difficulties; here is one such, an order to Justin, Lord Viscount Mount Cashel, master-gernal of the King's ordnance:

> Our will and pleasure is, that you forthwith deliver to the commissioners of the mint those two brass canons now lying in the court of this our castle marked &c weighing &c and for soe doeing this shall be your warrant. Given at our court at Dublin-castle this eleventh day of July, 1689, in the fifth year of our reign.[4]

The commissioners of the Capel Street mint in Dublin did not hesitate to take the initiative in obtaining suitable metal for coining, as this circular letter, written in 1689, indicates:

> Sir,
> We have great occasion for his majesty's use to procure as much hamered or forged copper and brass as your parts can afford, and judging by the decay of trade and desolation of the country, that there may bee a great deale in your district or port, we desire you, by yourself and officers, to inform us presently what quantity you may bee able to furnish us with, and what the currant prices are of each. And whatever you can gett, buy at the best rates you can, and as soon as you have four or five hundred weight, pray send it to us the commissioners of his majesty's minthouse in Capel-street, Dublin, and what you pay shall bee allowed you in your accounts at the custom house, so doing you'll oblige,
>
> Yours &c.[5]

Fascinating insight into the difficulties faced by metal collectors is provided in an amazingly frank letter written by one Wat Plunkett of Limerick. His letter dated January 4th, 1689, was sent to John Trindar, commissioner of the Dublin mint:

> Sir,
> Last Tuesday, the carriages parted from hence with six thousand six hundred weight of gunn mettle, six hundred a quarter and two pounds of fine pewter, and a thousand weight of steele, they will be eleven or twelve days a goeing because the roads are very deep – The pewter cost ten pence per pound, and steele six pence. You may expect very soone a farther supply of mettle for I have made an agreement with two eminent dealers from Corke who have five or six thousand weight of copper and brass which they are to send here. I must have an order from the lords of the treasury, for sending it to your mint; there are foure or five broken bells in the country, which I can have if you send an order for seizing them for the king's use; there is an useless cannon at Gallway, and one or two at Kingsaile; I forgot to send you some of our coyne as you desired, by the next occasion I will not faile; I cannot buy fine pewter now under eleven or twelve pence the pound, for they say that you give fourteen or fifteen pence in Dublin, the rates for carriage from hence to Dublin is eight shillings the hundred weight. I rest your humble servant,
>
> Wat Plunkett.[6]

A DATED GUN-MONEY SHILLING
The gun-money coins were dated by months, as well as years, probably to facilitate redemption on a date-order basis. Both large and small sizes of shillings were struck.

Despite many difficulties, the search for metal continued. The collectors were pleasantly surprised. Mint records show that over 200,000 pounds of metal were coined into sixpences, shillings, halfcrowns, and crowns with a face value of over £900,000. Initially the shillings and halfcrowns were struck on flans approximately the same size as corresponding English denominations but when metal became increasingly difficult to obtain, smaller pieces were struck.

Large and Small Gun-money Shillings

Thus, there were "large" shillings struck bearing months of issue in 1689 from July onwards, but for 1690 they cease with the month of April. In that month the striking of "small" shillings began, and continued to the month of September. April, 1690 is the only month which is represented by both sizes of shillings. Although the various proclamations of James do not offer an explanation for dating the gun-money series by months, the inescapable conclusion remains that he hoped to regain the crown and at that time would redeem the base coins for new ones issued with standard silver content. Thus, the shillings dated July, 1689 would have been redeemed first, those dated August, 1689, next, and so on.

After July, 1690, Dublin and its mint fell to William III and his army, but the mint at Limerick continued to strike shillings until September, and other coins until a month later. Limerick, in fact, was the last Irish city to resist the onslaught of William, not surrendering until October of 1691. Relatively few shillings were struck there after the fall of Dublin; those dated July to September, 1690, are the rarest of the series.

William lost no time in devaluing gun-money coins; a proclamation issued in July, 1690, from his camp near Dublin announced that henceforth the large shilling was worth only a halfpenny, and the smaller variety a farthing. Eventually the gun-money was prohibited altogether. With the halfcrowns and sixpences reduced also, anyone in Ireland with any quantity of these coins immediately found their value reduced to a minor fraction of their former worth. The resulting hardship and misery of the population is not difficult to imagine.

Today, almost two hundred years after the withdrawal of gun-money from circulation in Ireland, these intriguing coins remain popular with collectors. Like the currency of the Confederate States of America where another defeated people saw their money become worthless, the gun-money pieces tell a poignant story of a nation torn apart by opposing forces. Many gun-money coins have survived but, because they are struck in base metals, some are affected by corrosion or *verdigris*. However, searching for a set of shillings – including the large and small sizes with their months of issue – can be an exciting challenge.

EDINBURGH SHILLING

For three years in Queen Anne's reign the Edinburgh mint struck coin of the realm marked with an E; thereafter the mint closed, never to reopen.

Scottish Shillings

Unlike Ireland, Scotland produced few shillings of its own. There are only two basic types: a "miniature" shilling issued in the reigns of James VI (James I of England) and Charles I, and a shilling struck from English dies at the Edinburgh mint.

The tiny shilling was in silver and equal to one penny sterling.[7] It appeared about 1605 in the first coinage of James VI after he had become James I of England. Scottish pride came through in an order dated November 15, 1604 (following the King's accession to the English throne) which directed that the coins of Scotland be distinguished from those of England by having "ane special mark" – otherwise described as a thistle. The obverse of the little shilling has a rose with the old Tudor legend, ROSA SINE SPINA (A rose without a thorn) while the reverse bears (as directed by royal order) "ane thissel flowre." The inscription on the reverse was James' expressed hope of the benefits to be gained from the union of the kingdoms: TUEATUR UNITA DEUS (God upholds the united). This small, but attractive shilling continued to be issued in silver during the first decade of Charles I's reign; thereafter no distinctive shillings were struck in Scotland until the reign of the last Stuart, Queen Anne.

These last Scottish shillings appeared in the middle of Anne's reign and are distinguished from their English counterparts by the addition of the letter E or, in some instances, an E followed by a star. Puncheons and dies for these Edinburgh coins were sent to Scotland from the Tower Mint. The "E shillings" were issued for only three years – 1707, 1708, and 1709 – after which the Edinburgh mint was closed. Not until the 1937 shilling of George VI appeared with its Scottish reverse would the northernmost part of the United Kingdom again be honoured by a distinctive issue of the shilling.

Scottish Shilling Tokens

Although Scotland did not participate in the massive silver token issue of 1811–12, several Scottish shilling tokens did appear during the last decade of the eighteenth century. Dundee had a series of four tokens, the only one with a date being that issued by J. Wright, Junior, in 1797. For its obverse the token portrays the ruins of Broughty Castle; on the other side is an armed highlander encircled by the legend, FROM THE HEATH-COVER'D MOUNTAINS OF SCOTIA WE COME. Beneath the figure of the highlander, in an oval, are the arms, supporters and motto of Dundee. Three other Dundee shillings were also issued, each bearing the armed highlander, but with an obverse showing an ancient monument – long since dismantled. Unlike the 1797 token circulated by Wright, none of the other three Dundee shillings bears the name of an issuer.

Another Scottish shilling token was issued by Colonel William Fullarton in 1799.

DUNDEE TOKEN

J. Wright's attractive Dundee shilling (left) was issued in 1797. The reverse features a highlander ready for combat.

PRINCE OF WALES SHILLING

The 1799 Fullarton token (right) was so much like coin of the realm that it was not allowed to circulate.

Fullarton early in life achieved distinction in India for his military exploits. Returning to Britain, he represented several constituencies in Parliament. His remarkable shilling has a bust of the Prince of Wales on the obverse, and, for its reverse, a design very similar to that of George III's contemporary (1787) shilling. In addition to the shilling, Colonel Fullarton also struck halfcrowns and sixpences. When the Privy Council learned about the coins and their similarity to regal pieces, Colonel Fullarton was obliged to undertake that they would not be circulated. Nonetheless, a few specimens survived. Apart from their fine workmanship, they portray an excellent likeness of the Prince of Wales at the age of 37 when he was still more than two decades away from becoming king.

XIII
The Shilling in Other Lands

"The shilling was to circulate wherever the British drum was heard."
Robert Chalmers in *A History of Currency in the British Colonies.*

Robert Chalmers, who lived in the reign of Queen Victoria, envisaged the silver coinage of Britain being used throughout the Empire or, as he put it, "wherever the British drum was heard." While British coinage did not come to be used extensively abroad, Chalmers' statement was prophetic in the sense that many British colonies, the Dominions and, later, countries of the British Commonwealth, did, indeed, issue shillings (and other coins) in their own right. Thus a traveller circling the globe in the middle of the present century would have encountered shillings – most of them bearing the profile of the British sovereign – on the continents of Africa and Australia and in such widely separated places as Cyprus and Fiji, and New Zealand and New Guinea. But this traveller would have been surprised at the shillings that appeared in some newly independent nations of Africa in the 1960s. Instead of bearing the bust of the British monarch, they now rightly portray their national leaders together with fauna and flora of their respective lands.

The First Overseas Shilling

One is accustomed to think of the overseas shillings as emanating mainly from former British colonial territories and countries of the present Commonwealth, essentially in that area of the world containing Africa and Australia and the island areas between these continents. The first overseas shilling, however, circulated in a place far removed from this area – on islands off the coast of North America. It is to Bermuda, with its intriguing "Hog Money," that the honour goes for having the first shilling outside the British Isles. Records suggest the Hog Money shilling was put into circulation mid-way through James I's reign, about 1616. Bermuda originally had been part of the British colony of Virginia, but in 1614 the Virginia Company decided to relinquish the islands of Bermuda and pass them back to the Crown. It is interesting to speculate, had it not done so, that Bermuda could be an American state today. Eventually a new company was formed to deal exclusively with the territory of Bermuda. It bore an exceedingly long name: "The Governor and Company of the City of London for the Plantation of the Somer Islands."

The reason why Bermuda at that time was known as the Somer Islands derives from the extraordinary adventures of the English adventurer, Sir George Somers, who was shipwrecked there in 1609. (The spelling of the islands was sometimes Somer and on other occasions, Sommer; that which was to appear on the island coinage was incorrectly engraved as Sommer.)

In letters patent dated June 29, 1615, setting forth the rights of the new company, a special provision was made for coinage. ". . . Wee do further for us, our Heires and successors, give and Grant to the said Governor and Company, and their Successors," it read, "that they shall and lawfully Establish and cause to bee made a Coyne to pass

FIRST OVERSEAS SHILLING

The shilling (above) was one of four denominations issued in the reign of James I for the Somers Islands company. All four values have the same design: a hog on the obverse (hence "Hog Money") and a ship on the other side. The islands, present-day Bermuda, were colonized by Admiral Sir George Somers (right) whose name was misspelled on the coinage.

Currant in their said Somer Islands, betweene the Inhabitants there for the more easey of commerce and bargaining betweene them of such metall and in such manner and forme as the said Governor and Company in any of their said Generall Courts, shall limitt and appoint."[1]

If the foresight of the Somer Islands Company in providing coinage was remarkable, so, too, was its anticipation that the islands' inhabitants might resist using the coins. Such a concern, however, was not without foundation, for tobacco was by now an established commodity and islanders may well have preferred to use it as their medium of exchange. To preclude this possibility and to make clear the validity of the coinage, the Company issued an explicit instruction.

". . . we have appointed a base coyne, wch we send rated with our pvisions," the order read, "whereby you may give to such men there weekely wages when they worke, and as you shall find them to deserve, wth wch coyne yt shalbe lawfull and free for them to buy any pvisions out of the store, or any fishe, corne, tooles, or any such thinge in the Islands where they can gett the same. And to that end you shall pclaim the sayde coyne to be currant to pass freelye from man to man . . .."[2]

Compared with the English coins of James I, the Sommer Islands specimens were quite attractive. The obverse of the shilling, and its companion pieces, portrays the lowly hog together with the denomination in Roman numerals and the legend, SOMMER ISLANDS. On the reverse is a beautifully engraved sailing vessel flying the Cross of St. George from each of its four masts. The choice of the hog as a symbol of the islands was no accident; the Spanish explorer, Juan Bermudez, after whom the island group was later

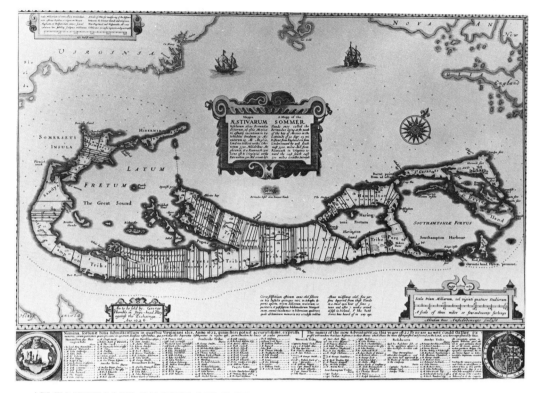

AN EARLY MAP OF THE SOMMER ISLANDS
Dated 1626, it contains many English place-names. The relative positions of
Virginia and New England are distorted on the map.

named, had come ashore a century earlier and left behind a few hogs which, during the
ensuing years, greatly multiplied. The new settlers, no doubt gratified at this unexpected
bounty of food, seized upon the animal as being singularly appropriate as a device for their
coins. The shilling is the highest denomination of the Sommer Islands coin series; other
values include the sixpence, threepence and twopence. All are extremely rare and few of the
surviving specimens are in good condition.

The Massachusetts/New England Shillings

During the latter part of Charles I's reign, the Commonwealth era, and the first few years of
Charles II's rule, there was an acute shortage of small change in New England. The Governor of Massachusetts, John Winthrop, remarked on some of the unpleasant circumstances
that arose from the shortage of coins. "The scarcity of money made a great change in all
commerce," he noted in his journal for October, 1640. "Merchants would sell no wares but
for ready money, men could not pay their debts though they had enough, prices of lands
and cattle fell soon to the one half and less, yea to a third, and after one fourth part." Then

PINE TREE SHILLING
This coin was struck in large
quantities in Massachusetts in the
middle of the seventeenth century.

he recounted a true story involving a man and his servant. "The wars in England," he said,
"kept servants from coming to us, so as those we had could not be hired, when their times
were out, but upon unreasonable terms, and we found it very difficult to pay their wages to
their content (for money was very scarce). I may upon this occasion report a passage
between one Rowley and his servant. The master, being forced to sell a pair of his oxen to
pay his servant his wages, told his servant he could keep him no longer, not knowing how to
pay him next year. The servant answered, he would serve him for more of his cattle. But
how shall I do (saith the master) when all my cattle are gone? The servant replied, you shall
then serve me, and so you may have your cattle again."[3]

John Hull Appointed Mintmaster

In 1652 the colony decided to act. The Massachusetts General Court designated John Hull
as the "master of the mint" and ordered him to start producing coins forthwith. Hull
enlisted the services of one Joseph Jenks to cut the first dies; the result of this labour was the
so-called "New England shilling." It did not compare well with the poorest of the English
hammered series. The flan was roughly cut and the design unimaginative and ill-
proportioned. The obverse bears only the initials NE (for New England) while the reverse is
equally austere, having only the numeral XII – the shilling's value in pence. As both these
inscriptions were small, the coin gives an appearance of being only half-struck on each side.

A coin with so little detail on it obviously lent itself to being counterfeited and John Hull
realized that these simple pieces would have to be replaced quickly by more sophisticated
specimens. After only four months, the New England varieties ceased to be struck, thereby
making them among the rarest of the early American coins. Besides the shilling, there were
New England sixpences and threepences – all dating from 1652.

Subsequently the Massachusetts General Court issued a new directive to John Hull in an
effort to thwart fraudulent coins being circulated. Henceforth, the Court said, the obverse of
coins should bear the inscription, MASSACHUSETTS, and the design of a tree enclosed in
a circle. The coin's other side, the order stated, should carry the words "NEW-ENGLAND
and the year of our Lord . . . ."[4] For the next thirty years coins were struck based on the
specifications of the Court's order. Nowadays this series is called "Pine Tree Money," but
numismatists – who have examined the pieces closely – tend to subdivide the group into
categories depicting three types of trees – willow, oak and pine. Besides shillings, the issues
included sixpences, threepences and twopences.

"[Although] the first money . . . [was] struck in 1652," writes an American historian,
"the same date was continued upon all that was struck for thirty years after . . .. No notice
was taken of it by the parliament [of Charles I] or by Cromwell; and having been thus

[facsimile of handwritten agreement]

SHILLINGS IN AN AGREEMENT WITH CAPTAIN MYLES STANDISH
Facsimile of an agreement between Edward Winslow and Captain Myles Standish involving the shilling (and pounds) in New England in January of 1627: "Edward Winslow hath sold unto Captain Myles Standish his six shares in the Red Cow, for and in consideration of five pounds ten shillings, to be pd. in corne at the rate of six shillings p. bushell, freeing the sd. Edward from all manner of charge belonging to the said shares, during the terme of the nine yeares they are let out to halves, and taking the benefit thereof."

indulged, there was a tacit allowance of it afterwards even by King Charles II for more than twenty years . . .."[5] Still, to be on the safe side, all the Massachusetts colony coins after the original issue bore the 1652 date. In this way the colonists could say their coins already existed should a king of England ever complain that the colonial pieces did not bear his profile and the royal arms.

The Pine Tree Shilling in Literature

During the time John Hull operated the mint in Massachusetts he did very well for himself. His first contract stipulated that he could keep eighteen pence out of every twenty shillings struck, or approximately $7\frac{1}{2}\%$ of the total value. Some people thought Hull was dishonestly striking coins for himself, but the General Court thought otherwise for they renewed Hull's contract year after year. Hull was a thrifty man who worked efficiently and during the long period when he produced the Massachusetts coinage, he earned a fortune. When his only daughter married, he is reputed to have presented a dowry of £30,000 – all in Pine Tree shillings. Nathaniel Hawthorne seized upon the wedding incident when he came to write the story of "The Pine-Tree Shillings" in *Grandfather's Chair* (see The Chronicles). Hawthorne did not cite the £30,000 figure, but did portray Hull offering his daughter's weight in Pine Tree shillings to the lucky husband, Samuel Sewell. Hawthorne also incorporated the Pine Tree shilling in another work of fiction, *The Great Carbuncle*, in which the miser, Ichabod Pigsnort, played with his shillings in almost childlike manner.

As late as the middle of the nineteenth century the Pine Tree shilling was still in circulation in parts of the United States. At that time its value, as recalled by a citizen residing in upper New York state, was 16 2/3 cents. "There everything was based on the shilling," he explained. "A quarter of a dollar was always 'two shillings' and all sums under 100 dollars

MARYLAND SHILLING

Lord Baltimore found himself in deep trouble for issuing this shilling and two other values bearing his own likeness when Maryland was still a colony of England.

were calculated on the same basis. When I asked the price of board, I was told it ranged from 16 to 30 shillings a week. The price of a suit of clothes was generally stated in shillings. That was all right for the natives, but I confess I had frequently to brush up my arithmetic to get at what 33 shillings, 22 shillings, 17 shillings or some other high number amounted to."[6]

Even though shilling coins may have disappeared from the American scene around 1850, the value was still used for reckoning in New York state as late as the 1930s. "I have heard old New York state farmers . . .," wrote a correspondent to *Country Life* magazine in 1971, "speak in terms of shillings [as recently as the 1930s], meaning a 'York Shilling' of 12 U.S. cents, equivalent until recently to the English 6d."[7]

Lord Baltimore's Maryland Shilling

But the story of North American shillings is by no means confined to the states of Massachusetts and New York. In 1658 another shilling appeared in the English colonies, this time in Maryland. Sixpence, fourpence and penny denominations were also issued. Cecil, Lord Baltimore, was the Lord Proprietor of Maryland, and he is generally believed to have personally approved the cutting of the dies of the Maryland coins. The pieces, both in design and workmanship, are far superior to those produced by John Hull in Massachusetts, no doubt because the dies were made in England, where Baltimore had access to good engravers.

The obverse of the shilling has a fine profile of Lord Baltimore facing left, with Latin legends giving his name, CAECILIVS, and that of the colony, TERRAE-MARIAE. Just in case the beholder of the coin missed the Baltimore association, he was reminded – when looking at the reverse – that he was gazing at the family's arms and its motto, CRESCITE ET MVLTIPLICAMINI (Increase and Multiply). The denomination's value is given in Roman numerals on the reverse. Charles II is said to have been furious when he was informed about the upstart coinage of Maryland bearing the bust of someone other than the royal personage. His Council of State immediately ordered the seizure of all dies, tools and equipment in England that had been used in striking the Baltimore pieces. For a period Lord Baltimore's own liberty was in jeopardy, but he managed to survive the episode and lived on to serve 43 years as Proprietor of Maryland. During all this time the English Civil Wars and other events kept him from setting foot in the colony. He entrusted the management of the colony's affairs to his younger brother, Leonard, who eventually became Maryland's first governor.

The "Good Samaritan Shilling" – A Spurious Issue

For many years numismatists admitted to the possibility of another North American shilling, the so-called "Good Samaritan" issue.[8] The principal device of this coin is a

THE GOOD SAMARITAN
This interesting shilling portraying the Good Samaritan purports to be a variety of the New England shilling, but after careful research, has been found to be a fake.

representation of the Biblical story of the Good Samaritan. Only two examples are believed to exist, one of which has the word FACSIMILE on it. An interesting feature of the pieces is their similarity in some respects to the Pine Tree shillings. After years of research an American numismatist, Eric Newman, concluded that both examples of the shilling are spurious. One example, known as the Pembroke specimen, is held by the British Museum, and the other, known as the Bushnell specimen, has been privately held since its discovery in the middle of the last century.

Token Shillings from Maryland and Virginia

As in Britain, tokens appeared in America during times when there was a shortage of change. At least two shilling tokens were issued, one in Maryland and one in Virginia. The Maryland token was struck under the authority of one John Chalmers, a goldsmith who resided in the state's capital, Annapolis. He first attempted to alleviate the coinage scarcity by dividing Spanish dollars into quarters. This practice he considered tedious and impractical, for the quartered sections hardly resembled that of conventional coins. Then he hit upon the idea of melting down Spanish dollars and making his own token coins – shillings, sixpences, and threepences. The designs were the same for all denominations: the obverse a simple declaration of the issuer's identity, I. CHALMERS ANNAPOLIS, and the reverse giving the other essential information – the coin's value, the date (1783) and a representation of a snake (or worm). Chalmers must have issued a fair number of these tokens, for varieties exist with snakes (or worms) of varying lengths.

The second token, probably a pattern since it is known only in brass, was issued for use by one Richard Dawson who lived in Gloucester County, Virginia. The obverse bears a pair of overlapping triangles which very much resemble the Star of David; around this device is Dawson's name. The other side portrays a building which may have been an early courthouse, or a warehouse for storing Dawson's merchandise. Beneath the building are the Roman numerals XII and around it is the token's provenance, GLOUCESTER.

Shillings of the Dominions

Over two hundred years were to elapse before a shilling was next to be struck by an overseas issuing authority: South Africa, in 1892. The coin was one of the series made at the state mint in Pretoria by the South African Republic (later Transvaal). The shilling is unusual in that it has no legend and only a portrait on the obverse. It is that of the Republic's president, S. J. Paul Kruger. The reverse has no design but merely lists the value, 1 SHILLING, the date, and the issuing authority, Z. AFRIK. REP.

After the Boer War, South Africa became a Union of four provinces: Cape Province, Natal, Orange Free State and the Transvaal. British coin of the realm was then imported

SOUTH AFRICA: FROM REPUBLIC TO UNION

Transvaal became the South African Republic, with Pretoria as its capital, in 1852. Under the presidency of Paul Kruger (shown at the left on his shilling) coins were struck in bronze, silver and gold. After the Boer War when the Union of South Africa was formed, the shilling depicted King George V (right).

FROM UNION BACK TO REPUBLIC

As the Union of South Africa, the country continued to reflect British sovereigns on its coinage. At the left above is the coin of George VI, while at the right is the shilling of Queen Elizabeth II. The Union came to an end in 1961. Again a republic, South Africa dropped the shilling when decimal coinage began.

and continued in use until 1923 when the mint at Pretoria produced a series of pieces ranging from the farthing to the sovereign. The shilling's obverse depicts a crowned King George V, while the reverse has an allegorical representation of Hope. Except for the profiles of later monarchs, the shilling's appearance was unchanged for the remainder of South Africa's status as a dominion – that is, until 1961.

Australia was the next Dominion to have shillings struck in its own name. The first were dated 1910, the last year of the reign of Edward VII, and bear the royal portrait on the obverse, and the national arms on the other side. Except for the change in bust, the shillings of George V are similar to the first issue. When George VI ascended the throne, the familiar arms portraying the kangaroo and emu were dropped, and a new one substituted depicting one of the country's prime agricultural resources – the Merino sheep. This animal continued on the shilling's reverse until 1966 when the coin – like its British equivalent – bowed to its decimal successor.

Maori Designs on New Zealand Shillings

The first New Zealand shilling was dated 1933. Its design changed little until the country instituted decimal coinage in 1967. The obverse always bore the bust of the reigning

AUSTRALIA: ITS ARMS AND ITS SHILLINGS

The arms (top, left) is found on the reverse of the country's shillings of Edward VII (top, right) and George V (centre, right). It consists of a shield bearing the badges of Australia's six states, and is supported by a kangaroo and an emu. When George VI ascended the throne, the arms was omitted and replaced by a symbol of the country's agricultural industry, the Merino sheep (bottom, left). The design was unchanged on Elizabeth II's coin (bottom, right).

monarch, the reverse a Maori warrior. When New Zealand changed to decimal coinage in 1967, the Maori theme for the shilling's reverse was retained – this time in the form of the tattooed face of a male, as depicted in traditional Maori carving. From 1967 to 1969 the shilling bore both the old value and its decimal equivalent, 10 cents, but ONE SHILLING was dropped from the coin in 1970.

Ireland had the same dominion status as Canada when its first modern shilling was issued in 1928. The reverse features a bull, one of several farmyard animals on a colourful series of coins. This shilling has the legend SAORSTAT EIREANN (Irish Free State) on its obverse, but when the country's political status was changed in 1937 and a new constitution adopted, the name was shortened to EIRE. Ireland retained the bull design on its shillings until its coins were decimalized in 1971.

THE MAORI OF NEW ZEALAND

All of New Zealand's shillings have featured the Maori warrior in one form or another. A warrior in war dance pose is shown above and is found on the reverse of shillings of George V (top, right), George VI (second, right), and Elizabeth II (third, right). The last shilling of Queen Elizabeth (bottom, right) depicts a Maori war mask.

Three island issuers of shillings, Cyprus, Fiji and New Guinea, present striking contrasts of design. The Cyprus coins were issued for only the years 1947 and 1949; both bear the effigy of George VI on the obverse and a heraldic pair of lions on the reverse. The Fiji piece is one of the most attractive of the overseas shillings. The monarch is on the obverse, but the other side portrays a picturesque native sailing boat. Fiji shillings were first struck in 1934. The third "island shilling," that of New Guinea, was introduced in 1935. It has a hole in the centre, a feature which precluded use of the royal portrait. The obverse has a crown above the hole and crossed maces beneath it. On the other side there is the value, date, and issuing authority, TERRITORY OF NEW GUINEA.

TWO VARIETIES OF IRISH SHILLINGS
The first Irish shilling, issued in 1928 (left) bears the Free-state term, SAORSTAT EIREANN, while the later issue used the modern name of EIRE (right).

THE FIJI SHILLINGS
Coins of George V and George VI are pictured above; those of Elizabeth II are similar except for the change in the monarch's portrait.

ISLAND SHILLINGS FROM NEW GUINEA AND CYPRUS
The New Guinea shilling (left) is the only one struck with a hole in it, thereby preventing the use of the monarch's bust. The Cyprus shilling was issued in only two years: 1947 (right) and 1949.

A Flood of African Shillings

All the remaining overseas shillings were struck for British territories in Africa, or newly established nations there. Just as the shillings of Britain reflect her history, so does the panorama of African shillings trace the growth and decline of British influence on the continent. The South African evolution from republic and colony to Dominion, and back to a republic has already been recounted; the dramatic changes in other parts of eastern, western and southern Africa is equally fascinating as revealed on shillings.

BRITISH EAST AFRICA
The two coins shown here, from the reigns of George V (above) and George VI (below) circulated in Kenya, Uganda, Tanganyika and Zanzibar from 1921 to the reign of Elizabeth II. In the 1960s they achieved independence and issued their own coinage.

Before the First World War the Indian rupee dominated trading in many parts of East Africa. When Tanganyika was added to the East African area after the war, a new, uniform currency was introduced based on shillings. The new (1920) set of coins included a shilling with the profile of George V (obverse) and a lion standing before a range of mountains (reverse). Except for the change in monarchs, this attractive shilling remained unchanged until Kenya, Uganda and Tanganyika (later, with the addition of Zanzibar, to become Tanzania) achieved independence and issued separate coinages.

Kenya's first shilling (1966) features the portrait of a man, Jomo Kenyatta, who became a national hero during the period leading up to independence. He defied the prediction of experts by uniting rival tribes. The legend around his effigy proclaims him as MZEE IOMO KENYATTA   THE FIRST PRESIDENT OF KENYA. The reverse bears the coin's value, date, national arms, and the words, REPUBLIC OF KENYA. One feature of the arms is the Swahili motto, HARAMBEE, meaning "self-help."

Uganda's first shilling also appeared in 1966 and is inscribed BANK OF UGANDA on both sides. The obverse bears the national arms and the coin's value; the reverse also gives the value and has a design similar to that of the old East African shilling with a background of mountains, but with a crested crane taking the place of the lion. Tanzania has its first president, Julius Nyerere, on its first conis, including the shilling. This set also appeared first in 1966. The reverse has a simple but striking device – the freedom torch.

West African Shillings

On the opposite side of Africa there was another large British territory originally known as British West Africa. It embraced what today are the independent nations of Nigeria, Ghana and The Gambia. Coinage based on sterling was used from the outset in this area.

The first British West Africa shilling was issued in 1913, although copper pieces were struck several years earlier. The profile of the British monarch occupies the obverse of the shilling and a familar West African sight – the palm tree – is on the reverse. This design remained virtually unaltered except for the change in sovereigns, for thirty-five years. The shilling was struck in silver up to 1920, but thereafter only in brass.

KENYATTA'S SHILLING
Kenya's first president, Jomo Kenyatta, is pictured on the obverse of
the country's shilling (right).

UGANDA'S CRANE
The reverse of Uganda's first shilling
(left) depicts an exotic crested crane.

TANZANIA PIECE
Julius Nyerere, first president, is
shown on the obverse of this 1966
shilling (right).

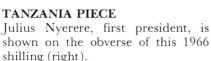

Ghana was the first of the former British West African territories to strike its own coins (1958). The design is uniform for the shilling and other denominations: a bust of the nation's leader, Kwame Nkrumah, on the obverse and a large star with the country's name, date, and value on the other side. Nigeria's national coinage started a year later (1959) when an attractive series was issued which features the profile of Queen Elizabeth II on the obverse and examples of the country's flora on the reverse. The shilling, like its West African predecessor, depicts an aspect (an arrangement of branches) of the palm tree. The reverse of the Nigerian shilling (and other values) incorporates mention of the federal system of government, CONFEDERATION OF NIGERIA – a structure that was almost destroyed during the civil war of the 1960s. For a short period the rebel state of Biafra tried to circulate coins, including a shilling, in aluminium. Dated 1969, the shilling has for its obverse a bird with outstretched wings, the date, and the words, REPUBLIC OF BIAFRA. The reverse portrays the familiar palm tree, this time silhouetted by the rising sun, and the legend, PEACE UNITY FREEDOM. When the Biafran independence effort failed, the coins were suppressed. The third independent nation to be carved out of the old British West Africa territory is The Gambia. It issued its own coins in 1966, of which the shilling bears the Arnold Machin bust of Queen Elizabeth II on its obverse, and a palm tree on the other side.

Central African Shillings

As varied and interesting as the shillings of east and west Africa are, it was to be the southern half of the continent which was to see some of the most exotic shillings ever struck.

THE CHANGING FACE OF WEST AFRICA

SHILLINGS OF BRITISH WEST AFRICA

These shillings circulated over a large area of West Africa in the first half of this century. At the left is a 1913 shilling of George V in silver; that at the right is of George VI in brass. In the 1950s and 1960s this area became the independent states of Nigeria, Ghana, and The Gambia.

GHANA AND THE GAMBIA

President Nkrumah is pictured on the obverse of Ghana's first shilling (left) while the Gambian shilling (right) has a cameo-like profile of Queen Elizabeth II.

SHILLINGS OF NIGERIA AND A DEFEATED BIAFRA

Nigeria, Africa's most populous nation, issued its own coinage starting in 1959. The shilling (left) bears the bust of Elizabeth II on its obverse. A decade later, another shilling (right) appeared when one region, calling itself Biafra, attempted to secede – and failed.

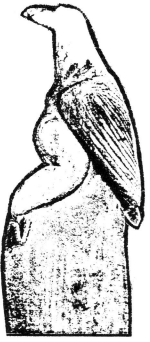

ZIMBABWE BIRD AND RUINS
Soapstone birds on pedestals were found in the ancient ruins of Zimbabwe (above) in the new African country of the same name, and formerly called Rhodesia. A bird was featured on coins of the new nation, as well as on Rhodesia's shillings.

Their issuance, however, has been accompanied by turmoil and violence – some of it extending right up to the present. The story of this last series of African shillings begins in 1932 when Southern Rhodesia issued coins for the first time. Prior to that year, South African coinage was in use. The 1932 Southern Rhodesia pieces also circulated in the adjoining territories of Northern Rhodesia and Nyasaland. The obverse of the shilling bears the profile of King George V and the reverse depicts the "Zimbabwe bird" – one of the relics from the fortress of Zimbabwe believed to have been erected by the Bantu people centuries ago. When the Central African Federation was later formed, a new coinage appeared (1955) embodying different designs. The royal profile still graces the obverse, but the reverse now depicts an elegant sable antelope. The Federation was short lived; by 1963 it had broken up. A year later Nyasaland became the independent nation of Malawi and Northern Rhodesia became Zambia. Both Malawi and Zambia now have their own currencies.

Shillings of Malawi and Zambia

The obverse of the 1964 Malawi shilling features its first president, Dr. H. Kamuzu Banda, and an arrangement of maize cobs on the other side. The Zambian shilling bears the national arms on the obverse and the hornbill bird on the reverse. Both Malawi and Zambia have now converted their coinage to the decimal system.

RHODESIA'S HISTORY TOLD BY ITS SHILLINGS

SOUTHERN RHODESIA'S SHILLINGS

The first coinage of Southern Rhodesia appeared in the reign of George V (left), followed by those of George VI (right). The reverse of these shillings depicts one of the soapstone Zimbabwe birds.

FROM FEDERATION TO INDEPENDENCE

When the next shilling (left) appeared in the reign of Elizabeth II, Rhodesia was a part of the Central African Federation. The country's last shilling (right) heralded the start of decimal coinage by listing the old shilling value and the new one of 10 cents. In 1980 Rhodesia disappeared from the map of Africa as the newly independent state of Zimbabwe was born.

With the break up of the Central African Federation, Southern Rhodesia became simply Rhodesia. It joined the other former members of the old federation by adopting decimal coinage in 1964. The shilling was altered very little, except for the substitution of the national arms for the Zimbabwe bird on the reverse, and the inclusion of both the old (one shilling) and the new (10 cents) values on its pieces. A year later Rhodesia declared itself independent of the United Kingdom government, but not of the monarchy. As a result of the Lancaster House Conference in 1980 Rhodesia became the independent state of Zimbabwe and subsequently new coinage was issued featuring the Zimbabwe bird on all denominations. With this new issue the term shilling was dropped from the 10 cents piece.

SHILLINGS OF MALAWI AND ZAMBIA
The first shilling of Malawi (formerly Nysaland) portrays Dr. Banda on its obverse
(left). Zambia's shilling (right) has its national arms for the obverse and a hornbill
on the other side.

Thus concludes the parade of African shillings, a series which began with a coin bearing
the profile of the president of the South African Republic in 1892, and ended with a variety
of shillings depicting presidents of newly independent African states. Taken as a group,
they form a nostalgic record of British administration on the continent and, later, its
displacement as territory after territory achieved statehood. It is ironical that although the
mother country, Great Britain, has dropped the shilling as an official unit of coinage, the
old value still lives on in some east African nations.

The Varied Fortunes of the Shilling

From the foregoing it is apparent that the shilling was more important in some areas of
British influence than others. Indeed, circumstances and geography were to affect its
acceptability.

In the New England states, for example, although pine-tree shillings were struck for three
decades and circulated much longer, the American preference for decimalized coinage and
the impetus for national currency following achievement of independence, meant the old
British values were doomed. By 1796 the United States mint was producing an entire range
of coins based on a decimalized dollar. The shilling was long since dead and remained only
as a unit of accounting in New York state.

For different reasons the shilling was not a feasible denomination for the Indian sub-
continent and places farther east. Native Indian coinage varied greatly from state to state,
and even when British coinage was adopted, wisdom dictated that the familiar rupee with
its divisions of the anna, pice and pie should be retained in preference to new denominations. Farther east, the dollar early became a favoured coin of commerce and by the latter
half of Queen Victoria's reign it had gained firm acceptance in the two great trading areas
of the Straits Settlements and Hong Kong. Thus, no shillings circulated in the vast expanse
separating Cyprus, the continent of Africa, and Australasia.

In the West Indies the state of coinage was even more complicated. At one time or
another copper farthings, halfpennies, and pennies were issued for use in Antigua, the
Bahamas, Barbados, and Bermuda. Fourpence pieces were struck for British Guiana and
the West Indies from 1891 to 1916 and for British Guiana alone from 1917 to 1945, but this
value was to be the nearest to a shilling the region would see. Another group of Caribbean
territories had first relied on whatever foreign coins they could obtain, sometimes
counterstamping or punching holes through them and, on occasion, even cutting them up

PLACES OUTSIDE BRITAIN
THAT HAVE ISSUED SHILLINGS

North America:
  Sommer Islands (Bermuda)
  Massachusetts/New England
  Maryland
  Annapolis, Maryland (token)
  Gloucester, Virginia (token)

Africa
  South Africa
  East Africa
  Kenya

Uganda
Tanzania
British West Africa
Nigeria
Biafra
Ghana
The Gambia
Southern Rhodesia
Rhodesia and Nyasaland
Rhodesia
Malawi
Zambia

Europe:
  Ireland
  Cyprus

Pacific Area
  Australia
  Tasmania (token)
  New Zealand
  Fiji
  New Guinea

into fragments. Latterly the area adopted decimal coinage with the 50 cents piece usually being the highest denomination issued.

Thus it will be seen that in Australia, New Zealand and in some parts of Africa the shilling survived longest. Why was this so? Practical considerations counted heavily: most trade was with the mother country, British coinage itself sometimes circulated in the regions, and some areas even had branches of the Royal Mint. But another explanation must be that British settlers, whose numbers grew steadily over the years, naturally preferred to retain the institutions with which they were most familiar – language, church, school, laws, customs – and the system of coinage.

The Customs

XIV
The Shilling in British Custom

"Cuppage accepted the . . . [shilling], accordingly, and was lawfully, enlisted . . . ."

Captain Dalston's journal, 1703.

"This is to certify that William Bowditch of South Petherton . . . was in a public house in Bridgewater . . . with his dealers selling shoes," reads an old Somerset document.[1] "J. Phillips, a recruiting sergeant belonging to the 13th Regiment of foot, a native of Broadwinsor in Dorsetshire, came into the said public house and, knowing each other, the said William Bowditch askt Phillips to drink a glass of gin with him, which he accepting and they thereupon being about to part, the said Phillips held out his hand desiring to shake him [Bowditch] by the hand, and having done so, a shilling dropt from between their hands, when Phillips at once swore that the shilling so dropt was to oblige Bowditch to serve his King George."

"But," the document continues, "it was proved that Bowditch never accepted or had the shilling nor did he know anything about it. However, as Bowditch was going to his standing in the fair disregarding the imposition of Phillips, the corporal attending Phillips ran after Bowditch, knockt him down, kickt him and dragged him back to the Inn where they confined him to a room, and treated him in a very barbarous, savage and inhuman manner, tearing his clothes from his back, his shoes from his feet, and his silver buckles from his shoes which are entirely lost."

Despite the unfair charge and the ensuing assault. Bowditch came out of the affair a free man. The Somerset magistrate who presided over the case explains why in the final words of his statement: "Wherefore and because the said Bowditch was thus trickt and trepanned and imposed upon and not duly enlisted by the said Phillips, the said Bowditch was by me discharged from the said Phillips. Given under my hand and seal this 14th day of March, 1778."

The Shilling in Military Recruitment

Bowditch was one of the lucky young men to escape the recruiting sergeant's wiles. Untold hundreds – if not thousands – of rural lads found themselves impressed into military service during the era when the practice of taking the King's (or Queen's) shilling was seldom challenged. The village dunce was easy prey for the sergeant who, attired in his impressive uniform, painted an exaggerated picture of life in the service of the monarch. Doubters were more difficult to convince, but they, too, often wilted under heavy drinking. Many awoke the morning after to find the tell-tale shilling in their pockets. This use of the shilling as a device to bind a man to enlistment is richly documented in British literature, drama, and folklore.

Perhaps the earliest recorded instance of a shilling being offered a recruit occurred at Cockermouth in Cumberland during the reign of Queen Anne. On June 1st, 1703, Captain Christopher Dalston noted in his journal that "at the house of Mr. John Inman in Cockermouth" he gave one John Cuppage, a fiddler by trade, a shilling, and that "Cuppage accepted the same, accordingly, and was lawfully listed by this informant." Captain Dalston recorded no untoward incidents in recruiting Cuppage and it is assumed the young recruit willingly entered upon military service.[2]

Although the shilling had considerable purchasing power in Stuart times, it would be a mistake to think of the coin as a bribe in recruiting. It was, rather, simply a visible means of agreeing on a contract and was derived from custom dating back to medieval days. "The payment of the King's, or Queen's shilling to a recruit on enlistment," states the Society for Army Historical Research, "was a survival of the medieval practice of paying earnest-money – 'God's penny,' it was often called – to bind a bargain. By accepting the shilling the recruit ratified and acknowledged the contract of service in the Royal forces into which he had entered."[3] Thus the custom of taking the shilling originally was a simple device for acknowledging a deal between two men and there is no doubt that it was accepted as such by both parties. But recruiting for the services was ever a competitive business with promise of reward in the form of favour or promotion for recruiters with best results. Abuse of the custom was inevitable and, in time, the passing of the shilling was called into question as being a sufficient legal basis to cause a man to give up his civilian status.

Recruiting Conditions Revised

Eventually the custom of taking the shilling had other conditions attached to it and the country rustic gained certain guarantees. The revised arrangement stipulated: "The acceptance of the shilling [came to be] ... treated as an agreement by the man to enlist, and [he was] either to complete his enlistment by attestation before a justice, [or] in default, to pay smart money, which latterly amounted to 20s. Enactments were made for giving him notice of what he was about to agree to, and for the lapse of a certain time between his receipt of the shilling, and notice, and his final attestation before the justice. On the other hand, if he absconded between his acceptance of the shilling and his appearance before the justice, he was liable to be apprehended as a vagabond, and punished accordingly, and also to be compulsorily attested as a soldier."[4]

By the end of Queen Victoria's reign the taking of a shilling as manifestation of voluntary enlistment was dead, but not before the custom had earned a permanent niche for itself in English social history. One author who helped to commemorate the custom was Charles Dickens who, in *Barnaby Rudge*, tells how young Joe Willet wavered between accepting and rejecting the awesome coin proffered by the smooth-talking Army sergeant. "[Willet] had courage . . .," Dickens recounted, "to resist all the affectionate importunities of the serjeant, who waylaid him at the door with many protestations of eternal friendship, and did in particular request that he would do him a favour to accept of only one shilling as a temporary accommodation." Alas, despite his initial caution, young Willet weakened the following morning and succumbed to the persuasion of the recruiting sergeant.

The Recruiting Officer: A Villain in Children's Literature

In the nineteenth century most children's books published in Britain had strong moralistic tones. If an author wanted to produce a best-seller for young people, all he had to do was to put together a collection of "dos-and-don'ts" with appropriate illustrations, and the book's success was assured. One such volume appeared in 1805 under the title, *Rural Scenes, Or A Peep into the Country for Good Children.* The author obviously felt the recruiting sergeant was a villain on the rural scene, for he deals with him severely. One sketch shows a country lad

THE COUNTRY LAD ABOUT TO BE ENLISTED

"Now, pray, my good fellow, don't let him persuade," implores the verse that accompanied this drawing from a children's book published in 1805. The shilling was the accepted sum for sealing the act of enlistment.

being proffered a shilling by a soldier while the drummer stands by in the background. A woman, perhaps the boy's mother (see illustration), looks on apprehensively from a nearby door. Beneath this poignant picture is this verse:

RECRUITING

"Now pray, my good fellow, don't let him persuade,
For shedding of blood is a very bad trade;
So back to your bus'ness, and follow your plough,
And honestly live by the sweat of your brow.[5]

The stratagems of the recruiting officer are best described in George Farquhar's play, "The Recruiting Officer," written in 1706. In it, Sergeant Kite makes great use of flattery in attempting to enlist Costar Pearmain. A typical passage:

[Kite]: If any gentlemen, soldiers, or others, have a mind to serve her majesty [Queen Anne], and pull down the French king; if any 'prentices have severe masters, any children have undutiful parents; if any servants have too little wages, or any husband a bad wife, let them repair to the noble Sergeant Kite, at the sign of the Raven, in this good town of Shrewsbury, and they shall receive present relief and entertainment. . . . Pray, gentlemen, observe this cap – this is the cap of honour – it dubs a man a gentleman in the drawing of a tricker; and he that has the good-fortune to be born six foot high was born to be a great man. Sir, will you give me leave to try this cap upon your head?

[Costar Pearmain]: Is there no harm in't? Won't the cap list me?

By the beginning of the third scene Sergeant Kite's tactics are beginning to have effect on Costar and his friend, Thomas. The action begins with Kite leading the drunken Costar onto the stage while the mob choruses:

"We shall lead more happy lives
By getting rid of brats and wives,
That scold and brawl both night and day –
Over the hills and far away."

The wily Kite then makes another flattering appeal:

"Hey boys! thus we soldiers live! drink, sing, dance, play; we live, as one should say – we live – 'tis impossible to tell how we live – we are all princes; why – why you are a king, you are an emperor, and I'm a prince; now an't we?"

The formula for successful recruiting thus had three elements: a glowing presentation of Army life, some device (usually strong drink) to make the country rustic more vulnerable, and the passing of earnest-money – usually a shilling.

Notwithstanding the often dubious and sometimes infamous recruiting practices of the eighteenth and nineteenth centuries, the institution of volunteering to serve one's country in uniform has survived. That it was derived from the strongest motives of patriotism is manifested by the large number of public houses in Britain which bear the name, "The Volunteer." Some have eye-catching signs portraying the farm lad being enlisted by the uniformed sergeant, and a few even show him accepting earnest-money in the form of a shilling.

Cutting off an Heir

In recent times another use of the shilling with legal ramifications became common – that of fathers leaving their heirs only a shilling so as to disinherit them. But long before this practice began, people mentioned shillings in their wills to achieve exactly the opposite purpose – that of symbolizing their love for relations or friends, or their respect for the parish church and local charities.

A typical such will was that of William Peacocke of Scotter, Lincolnshire, who died in September, 1644. After stating that he was "weake in bodie, but of good & perfect remembrance," he set forth the primary provision of his will. "First," he specified, "I give and bequeath my soule into the hands of God, my maker and redeamer, and my body to be buried in the church of Scotter aforesaid. As for my temporal goodes, I give and bequeath as followeth: Imprimis, I give and bequeath to John Peacock, my brother, twelve pence, intreating him, as ever there was love betwixt us, to be good and kind to my wife during her life, & that he would be pleased to let her have the house and farme I now live in for her naturall life before any other, for her rent, and desire him to be as father unto her."[6] The register of the Scotter parish church records that William Peacocke's widow lived on until 1661, and that the faithful John Peacock followed her to the grave nineteen years later.

Less than a century later the vindictive use of the shilling had become established. If a

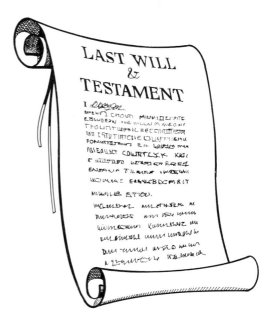

CUTTING OFF AN HEIR

A father, disappointed in his son, would leave him only a shilling in his will to indicate his displeasure.

son married against his father's wishes, was a wastrel, or in some other way had earned his parent's disapproval, the father – when he sat down to make his will – employed the shilling to demonstrate his feelings.

The vindictive father's method was simple: the erring son was bequeathed only a shilling. The reasoning behind such an act – no doubt justified in extreme cases – seems to have been this: if a will omitted reference to a son, the courts could conclude that he was simply overlooked; a shilling, however, was a specific sum (albeit a small one) and was taken as evidence that the father had given serious thought to the matter and had concluded that the son was not worthy of any greater inheritance.

Nonetheless the custom came to be regarded as despicable, and the courts did not always allow the force of such discrimination to take effect. Exactly when the practice was first instituted is unknown, but – like the taking of the shilling in military recruitment – it was well known in the eighteenth century. One particularly obnoxious case noted by the Law Society in the reign of George III, had a surprise ending.

"There is probably not to be found in any reports of the judgments of courts of law," records the Society, "a more striking instance of bad feeling by a father to a son than in the Scotch case of *Ross v. Ross*, decided by the Court of Session on 2nd March, 1770 . . .."

"Alexander Ross, solicitor, in London," the Society report continues, "made a will in 1748 by which he tried to disinherit his only son David [the first patentee of the Edinburgh Theatre Royal] . . .. As if it had not been enough to take such a step, he added insult to injury by giving his son a legacy 'of one shilling to be paid yearly on his birthday to remind him of his misfortune in having come into the world." The animosity which could dictate this is revolting and very likely unparalleled, but it is agreeable to know that, owing to its informality, the will was held to be ineffectual, and the son got his full right to all of which his father wished to deprive him."[7]

Like the custom of taking the enlistment shilling, that of cutting off an heir with a shilling

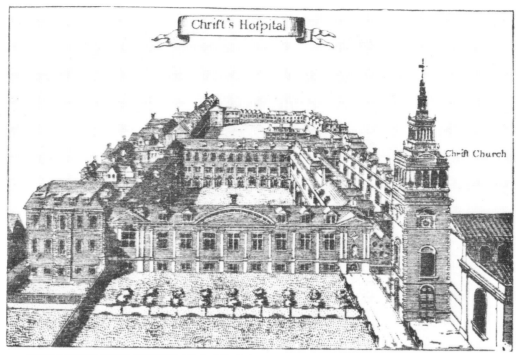

SHILLINGS FOR SCHOLARS OF CHRIST'S HOSPITAL
This old print shows Christ's Hospital when the public school was located in London. Each year scholars from the school, which is now in Horsham, go to Mansion House where they receive gifts of coins from the Lord Mayor. Formerly, shillings were among the coins distributed, but decimalization and inflation have resulted in coins of greater value being given. The custom dates back to the seventeenth century.

also found its way into the literature of Britain. Thomas Hood, in his three-volume novel, *Tylney Hall* (1834) refers to it, as does George Eliot in one of her best known works, *Silas Marner* (1861).

As late as the 1970s, wills were being proved with provisions for cutting off heirs with shillings. As demonstrated in the Scottish case cited above, courts have not always accepted the harsh wishes of the deceased – however much justification may have existed in the minds of those making the bequests. The reasoning perhaps lies in this Law Society comment: "The bequest of a shilling has long been considered the greatest testamentary insult that one human being can offer to another."[8]

Shillings for the Scholars of Christ's Hospital

One of Britain's oldest and most famous public schools, Christ's Hospital of Horsham (but formerly of London), takes part in an annual ceremony at the Mansion House in which the

Lord Mayor presents gifts of coins of several denominations. The custom dates back at least to 1681 and may be much older. It formerly took place on Easter Tuesday, but now occurs on St. Matthew's Day. In Anthony Trollope's day the scholars received sixpence each, the monitors a shilling, and the "Grecians" half a guinea.

When the school moved to Horsham the custom continued, with members making an annual pilgrimage to Mansion House where they were received by the Lord Mayor and presented with their coins. With inflation and decimalization the value of the Lord Mayor's gifts has increased; in the mid-1970s the scholars received the equivalent of three shillings (15 pence) and the monitors and other senior members also were given larger sums than before. It was the custom during the reign of William and Mary for the scholars to be served wine and buns at the presentation ceremony, but after a complaint by the Court of Aldermen of "great rudeness and disorders lately committed by the boys of Christ's . . . Hospital at Church time in Easter last (1693)," the imbibing aspect of the annual ceremony was dropped.[9]

The Citations

XV
The Shilling in Literature and Legend

"I have described in particular
What Twelve-pence *is, how it hath travell'd far;*
How to all ages, Sexes, Trades, and Arts,
It comes and goes, it tarries and departs . . . ."

John Taylor, in "A Shilling, or the Travailes of Twelve-pence."

Almost since the time when the shilling was introduced into the English system of coinage, it has appeared in works of literature either as a casual word of reference or as an actual subject of poets, essayists and diarists. A host of proverbs have emerged employing the shilling; unhappily, many of these will prove meaningless to future generations who are brought up on the decimal fivepence piece.

Probably the first person to commemorate the shilling in print was John Taylor, Britain's "water-poet." He was born in Gloucester during the reign of Elizabeth I, but gained his fame after he moved to London to become a waterman on the Thames. Here he styled himself as "The King's Majesty's Water Poet" and proceeded to produce an amazing variety of verses. He frequently drew upon his wide travels in choosing subjects for his poems. He was impressed into service in the Navy at an early age and saw action in Cadiz, but life at sea did not attract him. Returning to Britain, he became an inn-keeper, first in Oxford and later in London.

Perhaps Taylor's most notable exploit was to set for himself the task of travelling from London to Scotland without taking money, and without begging or borrowing funds. Determined to reach Scotland with these self-imposed restraints, he set out for the north, accompanied by a servant on horseback. What he lacked by not having a formal education he made up for in his rich store of adventures, a lively imagination, his robust good humour and extrovert personality. This combination of qualities endeared him to all he met, including Ben Jonson whom he encountered at Leith. Jonson was so bowled over by Taylor's simplicity of purpose and warm nature that he would not let the waterman depart without accepting a gold piece. When Taylor later sat down to record the adventures of his long trip to Scotland, he gave it the title of "The Penniless Pilgrimage, or the Moneyless Perambulation of John Taylor."

A Coin that Changed Hands Rapidly

The water-poet's journey to northern regions without means of finance led him to consider how easily a man might live without dealing in money, but merely by accepting payment in kind for services rendered. This line of thinking no doubt led him to realize how those with very little money must quickly part with it to survive. This, in turn, caused him to marvel how a popular coin (the shilling) changed hands so frequently among people of small means. In short, Taylor was inspired to write a remarkable poem entitled "A Shilling or, The Travailes of Twelve-Pence." The poem, which runs to many pages and is a fascinating commentary on the social conditions of the early Stuart period, is dedicated "To all those that have been, are, will or would be, Masters of a Shilling or Twelve-pence."

It begins by praising great voyagers such as Magellan, Columbus, Drake and others, but observes – despite their considerable achievements – ". . . if it be well considered, it will plainely appeare, that all their labourous endevours had an end with their lives. But the Travailer that I treate of, the thrice-trebble-tryumphant *Troynouantine Twelve-pence*, is like a perpetual motion in continuall travell, to whose journey there can be no end, untill the world come to a finall dissolution . . .."

Taylor, after flatteringly comparing the shilling with world renowned explorers, launches into his saga by relating how the shilling was born in a silver mine in faraway South America:

> From vast *America's* rude barbarous bounds,
> From rocky barren soyle, and sterril grounds,
> Where men did not their great Creator know,
> And where the *Devil's* the *God* to whom they bow,
> There from my Heathen *Dam*, or *Mother Earth*
> With paines and travaile, I at first had birth.

The poet then expounds on the difficulties experienced by workers in extracting the silver ore, in bringing it to civilization, and in converting it into bullion:

> With blood and curses I at first began,
> And ever since have been a curse to man.

Taylor writes that the choice of the name "shilling" was no mere accident for his wandering coin, as there were many foreign coins bearing attractive names drawn from Latin and other languages. All these were rejected, as were certain English denominations like the pound:

> A Shilling's much more auntient than a pound.
> And in pronouncing gives a better sound:
> As for example; which is most mouth-filling
> Of fifty pounds, or of a thousand shillings.

The "Water Poet" was aware that the shilling coin had existed since Tudor times, but he also knew that it had been a money of account long before that, as this next extract reveals:

> And though there scarce doth memory remaine,
> What I was e're the sixt King *Edwards* raigne,
> Yet before his time I was in value,
> As read in good true written stories shall you.

Next follows a detailed description of Edward VI's shilling, including references to the royal title and the religious legends (see also chapters devoted to Tudor and Stuart shillings). Taylor then lists the shillings which immediately followed those of Edward VI, reflecting the intense religious feelings which existed at the time:

JOHN TAYLOR (LEFT)
Britain's "water poet", and chronicler of a shilling's travels.

JOSEPH ADDISON
Addison (right) also wrote about the shilling's adventures.

And when my Master did respire his breath,
His sister *Mary*, and *Elizabeth*
Ordain'd new Twelve-pences with me to joyne,
But altred not my badge upon my Coyne,
Except a little which King *Philip* did,
Which Queene *Elizabeth* did soone forbid.

Taylor was staunchly patriotic and, taking from his pocket a shilling of James I and examining its reverse, he composed this verse to which he ascribed the subtitle, *Upon the Kings Armes.*:

Three Lyons Passant (borne by former Kings)
Subdues the Harp, quarters the *flowers* of *France*
Fourth Lyon Rampant, equall honour brings,
Through having power to warre doth peace advance,
United in great *James* this Royall stile,
King of great *Britaine*, *Fraunce*, and *Irelands* Ile.

At long last, after having established "my birth, my rising, my estate, my breeding," the shilling starts out on its never-ending journey. For page after page, Taylor recounts how the coin was first given by young men to a "loose woman" who, having contracted a "Frenchified heate" (the contemporary term for venereal disease), gave it to a surgeon who in turn passed it on to others, among them the apothecary, the tavern owner, wine merchant, market stall operator, the innkeeper, baker, miller, and eventually the thief.

He sums up the shilling's vagabond life by citing some of the things it will buy, and the advantages it holds over other denominations:

I have described in particular
What *Twelve-pence* is, how it hath travell'd far:
How to all ages, Sexes, Trades, and Arts,
It comes and goes, it tarries and departs:

I could tell further how it doth command,
In pressing men to serve by sea or land,
Now Bakers thirteene penny loaves doe give
All for a shilling, and thrive and live.
How it a pottle of good Clarret buyes,
How 'tis a quart of rich Canaries prise,
How far a thousand things 'tis daily ranging,
And is so round a summe, it needes no changing.

Other Shilling References

Although John Taylor is the first recorded literary figure to pay such extensive tribute to the shilling, English literature contains dozens of references to the coin – some brief, and others longer. It was a contemporary of the Water Poet, T. Cook Greene, in his *Tu Quoque*, who gave a formula for securing secrecy in a household: "A shilling to a servant that brings you a glasse of beere bindes his hands to his lippes."

The Irish writer, Jonathan Swift, referred in his letters to "Twelve Penny Weather," a term employed when the weather deteriorated to such an extent that it became necessary to hire a chair or a coach – for a shilling. Pure flattery perhaps best describes the assertion of Miguel de Unamuno, to whom is attributed the statement: "It is not the shilling I give you that counts, but the warmth that it carries with it from my hand."

It was a contemporary of Swift, the essayist Joseph Addison, who penned one of the most attractive accounts of the shilling. There must be few in the English-speaking world who did not get great pleasure from reading "Adventures of A Shilling," an essay which originally appeared in *The Tatler* (November of 1710), and later was reprinted in numerous anthologies of English literature. Schoolboys and schoolgirls who may have been bored by some works of great writers had no problem in following the astonishing adventures of the shilling coin as it passed from one person to the next. Addison himself summed up the magic appeal of the essay when he said: "we shillings love nothing so much as travelling." (The complete text of the essay may be found in "The Chronicles").

Robert Pollok, who died before he was thirty and barely lived to see the publication of his single great work, *The Course of Time*, wrote in the style of Milton. Some of his writing reads like a tedious sermon, replete with admonition after admonition. One reference involving the shilling bluntly points out a common frailty of man:

With one hand he put
A penny in the urn of poverty
And with the other took a shilling out.

Sir Walter Scott reminds us of one of the oldest adages when, in his *Redgauntlet*, he warns that bad characters "will come back, like an ill shilling." Benjamin Franklin, the American writer, inventor and diplomat, was noted for his blunt tongue. In a letter to his friend, Benjamin Vaughan, he noted that "a shilling spent by a fool may be picked up by a wiser person."

One of the first American novelists, Nathaniel Hawthorne, lived at the time when one of the most famous of shillings – the "Pine Tree Shilling" of New England – was in circulation. It was natural that some of his literary works should mention this attractive coin and

KIPLING'S STUDY
Here at Bateman's, near Burwash in Sussex, the Nobel Prize winner for literature wrote some of his best known works. Among his *Barrack Room Ballads* is "Shillin' A Day," a lament on the pension the British soldier received in the time of Queen Victoria.

one of them, "The Pine-Tree Shillings" (see "The Chronicles"), centres around these early pieces.

Use of the Term "Bob" for a Shilling

Pierce Egan (1772–1849), whose book, *Life in London*, took Britain by storm in 1821, records one of the earliest uses of the slang term "bob" for a shilling. *Life in London*, subtitled "The Day and Night Scenes of Jerry Hawthorn, Esq., and His Elegant Friend, Corinthian Tom, Accompanied by Bob Logic, the Oxonian, in Their Rambles and Sprees through the Metropolis," was a sensation because of its lively style and Egan's clever mixture of scenes from high and low life. In this classic satire he was ably abetted by the Cruikshanks, J.R. and George, whose engravings lend a further zest to this biting commentary of the times. A Cruikshank drawing shows the group at the Royal Academy where Bob Logic concludes the price of admission "is a bob well laid out." To this pronouncement Tom replies: "I agree with you, Logic; it is, I think, not only one of the cheapest but the best shilling's worth in London . . .." Just when "bob" was first used for the shilling is unknown, but one theory is that it originated during Sir Robert Walpole's term as Prime Minister (hence "bob" for Robert). It appears in an obscure reference work in 1812, was employed by Charles Dickens in *The Pickwick Papers*, and has turned up in numerous works of fiction since. Among the archives of the Royal Mint is the account of a court case in 1825 involving counterfeited coins. John Elledge, one of the principals in the case, refers in his testimony to "two-score of *bobs*, (I meant shillings)." This reference suggests that the use of bob for shilling was well established by 1825, but nonetheless required a more precise identification in a court of law.

Thomas Hood Champions the Sunday Zoo

In a stanza of his "An Open Question," the poet Thomas Hood (1799–1845) incidentally refers to the shilling while striking a blow for keeping the London Zoo open on Sundays:

What, shut the Gardens! lock the lattice gate!
Refuse the shilling and the Fellow's ticket!
. . . .
Now, really, this appears the common case
Of putting too much Sabbath into Sunday –
But what is your opinion, Mrs. Grundy?

The winner of the 1907 Nobel prize for literature, Rudyard Kipling, also devoted an entire poem to the shilling. Renowned for his earthiness and sympathetic portrayal of the soldier's life, Kipling describes the dismal future of the then-poorly paid British Tommy in "Shillin' A Day," taken from his popular *Barrack Room Ballads:*

. . . I'm old and I'm nervis,
I'm cast from the Service,
And all I deserve is a shillin' a day.

After this, and other verses, follows the refrain:

Shillin' a day,
Bloomin' good pay –
Lucky to touch it, a shillin' a day.

The younger generation has not been overlooked in references to the shilling, thanks to the pen of Edward Lear. Even if the shilling is destined to disappear, Lear's charming account of how Piggy-wig was deprived of the ring at the end of his nose will live on in the minds and hearts of young people:

'Dear Pig, are you willing to sell for one shilling
Your ring?' Said the Piggy, 'I will.'
So they took it away, and were married next day
By the turkey who lives on the hill.

The Shilling in Proverbs

Aside from its solid place in literature, the shilling long has been a favourite subject for proverbs.[1] Some sayings date back to the coin's origin in Tudor times; John Heywood gave this advice to help strike a bargain on market day: "He maketh his marks with marchantis likely to brynge a shilling to IX pens quickly." In more recent times other proverbs also emphasize the value of the twelve-penny piece: "Better give a shilling than lend a half-crown," and "You may know by a penny how a shilling spends." Occasionally, the shilling has turned up to describe the seamy side of life. A strong drink which caused burning sensations in the throat was said to make the imbiber "spit shillings," and – in lighter vein – there was an expression used to describe the village half-wit. If he was said to be "about nine pence in the shilling," he definitely was not all there.

The Chronicles

Adventures of a Shilling

By Joseph Addison

[The essay below, which appeared in *The Tatler* on 11 November 1710, has been a favourite in the English-speaking world for almost three centuries. Addison (1672–1719), a foremost numismatist of his day, traces the birth of the "talking" shilling from a silver mine in Peru to its reincarnation (after being melted down) as a shilling of Queen Anne.]

Per varios casus, per tot discrimina rerum,

Tendimus. – VIRG.

Through various hazards and events we move.   DRYDEN.

From my own Apartment, November 10.

I was last night visited by a friend of mine, who has an inexhaustible fund of discourse, and never fails to entertain his company with a variety of thoughts and hints that are altogether new and uncommon. Whether it were in complaisance to my way of living, or his real opinion, he advanced the following paradox, "That it required much greater talents to fill up and become a retired life, than a life of business." Upon this occasion he rallied very agreeably the busy men of the age, who only valued themselves for being in motion, and passing through a series of trifling and insignificant actions. In the heat of his discourse, seeing a piece of money lying on my table, "I defy (says he) any of these active persons to produce half the adventures that this twelvepenny piece has been engaged in, were it possible for him to give us an acount of his life."

My friend's talk made so odd an impression upon my mind, that soon after I was a-bed I fell insensibly into a most unaccountable reverie, that had neither moral nor design in it, and cannot be so properly called a dream as a delirium.

Methought the shilling that lay upon the table reared itself upon its edge, and turning the face towards me, opened its mouth, and in a soft silver sound, gave me the following account of his life and adventures:

"I was born (says he) on the side of a mountain, near a little village of Peru, and made a voyage to England in an ingot, under the convoy of Sir Frances Drake. I was, soon after my arrival, taken out of my Indian habit, refined, naturalised, and put into the British mode, with the face of Queen Elizabeth on one side, and the arms of the country on the other. Being thus equipped, I found in me a wonderful inclination to ramble, and visit all parts of the new world into which I was brought. The people very much favoured my natural disposition, and shifted me so fast from hand to hand, that before I was five years old, I had travelled into almost every corner of the nation. But in the beginning of my sixth year, to my unspeakable grief, I fell into the hands of a miserable old fellow, who clapped me into an iron chest, where I found five hundred more of my own quality who lay under the same confinement. The only relief we had, was to be taken out and counted over in the fresh air every morning and evening. After an imprisonment of several years, we heard somebody knocking at our chest, and breaking it open with a hammer. This we found was the old man's heir, who, as his father lay a dying, was so good as to come to our release; he separated us that very day. What was the fate of my companions I know not; as for myself, I was sent to the apothecrary's shop for a pint of sack. The apothecary gave me to an herb-woman, the herb-woman to a butcher, the butcher to a brewer, and the brewer to his wife, who made a present of me to a nonconformist preacher. After this manner I made my way merrily through the world, for, as I told you before, we shillings love nothing so much as travelling. I sometimes fetched in a shoulder of mutton, sometimes a play-book, and often had the satisfaction to treat a Templar at a twelvepenny ordinary, or carry him, with three friends, to Westminster Hall.

"The midst of this pleasant progress, I was arrested by a superstitious old woman, who shut me up in a greasy purse, in pursuance of a foolish saying, 'That while she kept a Queen Elizabeth shilling about her, she should never be without money.' I continued here a close prisoner for many months, till at last I was exchanged for eight and forty farthings.

"I thus rambled from pocket to pocket till the beginning of the civil wars, when, to my shame be it spoken, I was employed in raising soldiers against the king, for being of a very tempting breadth, a sergeant made use of me to inveigle country fellows, and list them in the service of the parliament.

"As soon as he had made one man sure, his way was to oblige him to take a shilling of a more homely figure, and then practice the same trick upon another. Thus I continued doing great mischief to the crown, till my officer, chancing one morning to walk abroad earlier than ordinary, sacrificed me to his pleasures, and made use of me to bestow me on a milk-maid. This wench bent me, and gave me to her sweetheart, applying more properly than she intended the usual form of, 'To my love and from my love.' This ungenerous gallant marrying her within a few days after, pawned me for a dram of brandy, and drinking me out next day, I was beaten flat with a hammer, and again set a running.

"After many adventures, which it would be tedious to relate, I was sent to a young spendthrift, in company with the will of his deceased father. The young fellow, who I found was very extravagant, gave great demonstrations of joy at the receiving of the will, but opening it, he found himself disinherited and cut off from the possession of a fair estate, by virtue of my being made a present to him. This put him into such a passion, that after having taken me in his hand, and cursed me, he squirred me away from him as far as he could fling me. I chanced to light in an unfrequented place under a dead wall, where I lay undiscovered and useless, during the usurpation of Oliver Cromwell.

"About a year after the king's return, a poor cavalier that was walking there about dinner-time, fortunately cast his eye upon me, and, to the great joy of us both, carried me to a cook's shop, where he dined upon me, and drank the king's health. When I came again into the world, I found that I had been happier in my retirement than I thought, having probably, by that means, escaped wearing a monstrous pair of breeches.

"Being now of great credit and antiquity, I was rather looked upon as a medal than an ordinary coin, for which reason a gamester laid hold of me, and converted me to a counter, having gotten together some dozens of us for that use. We led a melancholy life in his possession, being busy at those hours wherein current coin is at rest, and partaking the fate of our master, being in a few moments valued at a crown, a pound, or a sixpence, according to the situation in which the fortune of the cards placed us. I had at length the good luck to see my master break, by which means I was again sent abroad under my primitive denomination of a shilling.

"I shall pass over many other accidents of less moment, and hasten to that final catastrophe, when I fell into the hands of an artist, who conveyed me under ground, and with an unmerciful pair of shears, cut off my titles, clipped my brims, retrenched my shape, rubbed me to my inmost ring, and, in short, so spoiled and pillaged me, that he did not leave me worth a groat. You may think what a confusion I was in, to see myself thus curtailed and disfigured. I should have been ashamed to have shown my head, had not all my old acquaintance been reduced to the same shameful figure, excepting some few that were punched through the belly. In the midst of this general calamity, when everybody thought our misfortune irretrievable, and our case desperate, we were thrown into the furnace together, and (as it often happens with cities rising out of a fire) appeared with greater beauty and lustre than we could ever boast of before. What has happened to me since this change of sex which you now see, I shall take some other opportunity to relate. In the mean time, I shall only repeat two adventures, as being very extraordinary, and neither of them having ever happened to me above once in my life. The first was, my being in a poet's pocket, who was so taken with the brightness and novelty of my appearance, that it gave occasion to the finest burlesque poem in the British language, entitled from me, 'The Splendid Shilling.' The second adventure, which I must not omit, happened to me in the year 1703, when I was given away in charity to a blind man, but indeed this was by mistake, the person who gave me having heedlessly thrown me into the hat among a pennyworth of farthings."

The Pine-Tree Shillings

By Nathaniel Hawthorne

[In *Grandfather's Chair*, from which this extract is taken, Nathaniel Hawthorne (1804–64) relates how the mintmaster of Massachusetts, Captain John Hull, came to give his son-in-law thousands of Pine-Tree shillings on the occasion of his daughter's marriage. Hull, indeed, was the mintmaster of Massachusetts (see the chapter on overseas shillings), but it is likely that the romance described by Hawthorne owes more to fancy than fact.]

The Captain John Hull ... [previously mentioned] was the mintmaster of Massachusetts, and coined all the money that was made there. This was a new line of business, for in the earlier days of the colony, the current coinage consisted of gold and silver money of England, Portugal, and Spain. These coins being scarce, the people were often forced to barter their commodities instead of selling them.

For instance, if a man wanted to buy a coat, he perhaps exchanged a bear skin for it. If he wished for a barrel of molasses, he might purchase it with a pile of pine boards. Musket bullets were used instead of farthings. The [American] Indians had a sort of money, called wampum, which was made of clam shells, and this strange sort of specie was likewise taken in payment of debts by the English settlers. Bank bills had never been heard of. There was not money enough of any kind, in many parts of the country, to pay the salaries of the ministers, so that they sometimes had to take quintals of fish, bushels of corn, or cords of wood, instead of silver or gold.

As the people grew more numerous, and their trade one with another increased, the want of current money was still more sensibly felt. To supply the demand, the general court passed a law for establishing a coinage of shillings, sixpences and threepences. Captain John Hull was appointed to manufacture this money, and was to have about one shilling out of every twenty to pay him for the trouble of making them.

Hereupon all the old silver in the colony was handed over to Captain John Hull. The battered silver cans and tankards, I suppose, and silver buckles, and broken spoons, and silver buttons of wornout coats, and silver hilts of swords that had figured at court – all such curious old articles were doubtless thrown into the melting pot together. But by far the greater part of the silver consisted of bullion from the mines of South America, which the English buccaneers – who were little better than pirates – had taken from the Spaniards, and brought to Massachusetts.

All this old and new silver being melted down and coined, the result was an immense amount of splendid shillings, sixpences and threepences. Each had the date, 1652, on the one side, and the figure of a pine-tree on the other. Hence they were called pine-tree shillings. And for every twenty shillings that he coined, you will remember, Captain John Hull was entitled to put one shilling in his own pocket.

The magistrates soon began to suspect that the mintmaster would have the best of the bargain. They offered him a large sum of money if he would but give up that twentieth shilling which he was continually dropping into his own pocket. But Captain Hull declared himself perfectly satisfied with the shilling. And well he might be, for so diligently did he labour, that, in a few years, his pockets, his money bags, and his strong box were overflowing with pine-tree shillings. This was probably the case when he came into possession of Grandfather's chair, and, as he had worked so hard at the mint, it was certainly proper that he should have a comfortable chair to rest himself in.

When the mintmaster had grown very rich, a young man, Samuel Sewell by name, came a-courting to his only daughter. His daughter – whose name I do not know, but we will call her Betsey – was a fine, hearty damsel, by no means so slender as some young ladies of our own days. On the contrary, having always fed heartily on pumpkin pies, dough-nuts, Indian puddings, and other Puritan dainties, she was as round and plump as a pudding herself. With this round, rosy Miss Betsey did Samuel Sewell fall in love. As he was a young man of good character, industrious in his business, and a member of the church, the mintmaster very readily gave his consent.

"Yes, you may take her," said he, in his rough way, "and you'll find her a heavy burden enough!"

On the wedding day, we may suppose that honest John Hull dressed himself in a plum-coloured coat, all the buttons of which were made of pine-tree shillings. The buttons of his waistcoat were sixpences, and the knees of his smallclothes were buttoned with silver threepences. Thus attired, he sat with great dignity in Grandfather's chair, and being a portly old Gentleman, he completely filled it from elbow to elbow. On the opposite side of the room, between her bridesmaids, sat Miss Betsey. She was blushing with all her might, and looked like a full-blown peony, or a great red apple.

There, too, was the bridegroom, dressed in a fine purple coat and gold lace waistcoat, with as much other finery as the Puritan laws and customs would allow him to put on. His hair was cropped close to his head, because Governor Endicott had forbidden any man to wear it below the ears. But he was a very personable young man, and so thought the bridemaids and Miss Betsey herself.

The mintmaster also was pleased with his new son-in-law, especially as he had courted Miss Betsey out of pure love, and had said nothing at all about her portion. So, when the marriage ceremony was over, Captain Hull whispered a word to two of his men servants, who immediately went out, and soon returned, lugging in a large pair of scales. They were such a pair as wholesale merchants use for weighing bulky commodities, and quite a bulky commodity was now to be weighed in them.

"Daughter Betsey," said the mintmaster, "get into one side of those scales."

Miss Betsey – or Mrs. Sewell, as we must now call her – did as she was bid, like a dutiful child, without any question of the why and wherefore. But what her father could mean, unless to make her husband pay for her by the pound (in which case she would have been a dear bargain), she had not the least idea.

"And now," said honest John Hull to the servants, "bring that box hither."

The box to which the mintmaster pointed was a huge, square, iron bound, oaken chest; it was big enough, my children, for all four of you to play at hide-and-seek in. The servants tugged with might and main, but could not lift this enormous receptacle, and were finally obliged to drag it across the floor. Captain Hull then took a key from his girdle, unlocked the chest, and lifted its ponderous lid. Behold! It was full to the brim of bright pine-tree shillings, fresh from the mint, and Samuel Sewell began to think that his father-in-law had got possession of all the money in the Massachusetts treasury. But it was only the mintmaster's honest share of the coinage.

Then the servants, at Captain Hull's command, heaped double handfuls of shillings into one side of the scales, while Betsey remained in the other. Jingle, jingle, went the shillings, as handful after handful was thrown in, till, plumpy and ponderous as she was, they fairly weighted the young lady from the floor.

"There, son Sewell!" cried the honest mintmaster, resuming his seat in Grandfather's chair, "take these shillings for my daughter's portion. Use her kindly, and thank Heaven for her. It is not every wife that's worth her weight in silver!"

The Last Shilling Soldier

by Richard K. Brunner

[This true story, written in the 1970s, first appeared in the international newspaper, *The Christian Science Monitor*. It tells how an American, about to return home from London, visits a toy shop and spends his last shilling for a little soldier – a present for his daughter.]

"Daddy, tell me about the Last Shilling Soldier!"

A brilliant burst of left-over Indian summer sunlight pierces the December gloom, cutting between the organdy curtains like a stripe on a regimental flag. My daughter is speaking but it is the clipped precise English voice of a guards officer I hear, admonishing me – when I was asking about the markings on his regimental *flag* – "Never call it a flag. Regimental *Colour*, that's the proper form."

My daughter has heard the tale often enough. But once again I fold her into my arms (it is just barely comfortable to do so) and begin to recount events of a December morning years ago in London.

The graceful sweep of Regent Street and the spoke of Piccadilly float into focus, and I see myself rushing about on last minute errands before a dash to the airport and westward flight home across the Atlantic. The 6-inch military gentleman in question (now standing sentry near the very Pennsylvania fields his red coated comrades-in-arms tramped over when George III was King of America) was purchased with the last shilling I would ever spend in England. For, by my next visit, the noble shilling had been replaced by a decimal impostor known, inelegantly, as 5 New Pence.

I discovered the Last Shilling Soldier in a shop where, years before, I had found a pair of Dickensian characters in clay – the improvident optimist, Wilkins Micawber, and the sadistic schoolmaster, Wackford Squeers.

The soldier was not window-dressing fare. Dust was trapped in his plumeless bearskin, and he stood on an open shelf, conspicuous mercantile evidence that, at 30 shillings, this bit of tin and paint was not worth locking up behind glass. Perhaps it was this, and the rakish

168

set of his eyebrows and the red of his tunic – rather the colour found in a child's old-fashioned paintbox – that drew me to him. Clearly the stamp of the playing fields of Eton was not upon him; he could have been a Yorkshireman, or, as easily, a Cockney who hears Bow Bells every morning of his youth.

Not long after the Last Shilling Soldier took up his post on a shelf in my daughter's room, a book on obscure military uniforms arrived from an Edinburgh bookseller. This my daughter consulted diligently, hoping to discover a clue to her guardian's gladiatorial derivation. Finally, she announced that the Last Shilling Soldier belonged to no recognized regiment. No well-turned-out brigade would claim him, no renegade battalion would list him on its duty roster. Indeed her researches brought her to the conclusion that the Last Shilling Soldier was a one-man army.

It is precisely this isolation that marks him splendid; it conjures up a pretend-regiment comprised of every soldier ever in Britannia's service. His countenance, sold as a half crown minted when the young Victoria slept in Buckingham Palace, suggests a panorama of British martial history. Surely the Last Shilling Soldier was with Henry V on St. Crispin's Day, 1415, at Agincourt; marched with Marlborough's men at Blenheim, and stood with Wellington at Waterloo on that June day in 1815 that put paid to the Napoleonic era. His boots have trod the slosh of Sebastopol and the paving stones of Birdcage Walk.

It is not, however, the Last Shilling Soldier's past military feats which most enchant my daughter – rather it is his loyal service since his arrival. For "Daddy, tell me about the Last Shilling Soldier" has become our catchphrase when we wish to retreat. It is he who brings us to sit in the twilight of angry winter afternoons, snug and cozy behind drawn drapes, and over cups of chocolate, [we] conduct grown-up conversation about why clowns are sad and soldiers brave and rag dolls gay: father and daughter companionable contemporaries, though separated by half a lifetime of years.

Days pass. The Last Shilling Soldier stands his post, between Oliver Twist and Mr. Bumble, guarding the doorway, patient for those moments when a child's hands caress him and quiet voice comforts him in the wake of lost battles and diminished empire.

Then comes a morning early in December. "Daddy, tell me about the Last Shilling Soldier." And once again the magic begins. The rush of Regent Street. Seeking out the toy shop. The crisp morning air. I hurry beneath the fixed gaze of turtle doves perched on wire above the roadway, part of the street's Christmastide regalia. A No. 12 bus glides to a stop. I see the faces of the people in the queue clearly. I approach the shop – between a travel agency and a bespoke shirtmaker's. It is at the jingle of the shopbell that I realize all is not well. Not in Regent Street but in Pennsylvania. My daugher is not attending. Her thoughts are elsewhere engaged.

My voice moves the narrative along its familiar pathway, all the while my brain is trying to work out what's amiss. When it comes to me my voice falters. The story has become more important for me to tell than for her to listen to. How long she has known this I cannot say. But for that charitable insight, for knowing how to give such innocent pleasure to her father, I love her all the more.

Today the Last Shilling Soldier no longer reminds me of a morning years ago in London, but of a daughter's unexpected, wondrous gift.

BIBLIOGRAPHY

Brooke, G. C., *English Coins*. 3rd edn., 1932. Reprinted 1950, 1966.

Challis, C. E., *The Tudor Coinage* (Manchester, 1978).

Chalmers, Robert, *A History of Currency in the British Colonies*. 1893.

Crosby, S. S., *The Early Coins of America*. 1875. Reprinted 1974.

Craig, Sir John, *The Mint*. 1953.

Dalton, Richard, *The Silver Token Coinage Mainly Issued between 1811 and 1812*. 1922. Reprinted 1968.

Davis, W. J., *The Nineteenth Century Token Coinage of Great Britain, Ireland, the Channel Islands and the Isle of Man*. 1904. Reprinted 1969.

Dowle, A. and Finn, P., *The Guidebook to the Coinage of Ireland from 995 A.D. to the Present Day*. 1969.

Dyer, G. P., *The Proposed Coinage of King Edward VIII*. 1973.

Grierson, Philip, "Notes on Early Tudor Coinage" (*BNJ*, 1971), pp. 80–94.

Grueber, H. A., *Handbook of the Coins of Great Britain and Ireland in the British Museum*. 1899. Revised 1970.

Hanley, Tom and James, Bill, *Collecting Australian Coins*. (n.d.)

Hawkins, E., *The Silver Coinage of England*. 1887. Reprinted 1970.

Hsun, L. Ming, *The Great Recoinage of 1696–9*. 1966.

Jossett, C. R., *Money in Britain*. 1971.

Linecar, H., *The Milled Coinage of England, 1662–1946*. Supplement to 1958. 1966.

Mathias, P., *English Trade Tokens: The Industrial Revolution*. 1962.

Nelson, P., "The Obsidional Money of the Great Rebellion, 1642–9." *BNJ* ii, p. 291.

——, "Notes on the Great Recoinage of William III." *BNJ* iii, p. 223.

——, *Coinage of Ireland in Copper, Tin and Pewter, 1460–1826*. 1905.

North, J. J., *English Hammered Coinage* (II, Edward I–Charles II). 1976.

Oman, Sir Charles, *The Coinage of England*. 1931. Reprinted 1967.

Pridmore, F., *The Coins of the British Commonwealth of Nations to the End of the Reign of George VI*. Pt. I (Europe) 1952; Pt. II (Asia) 1965.

Remick, J., James, S., Dowle, A., and Finn, P., *British Commonwealth Coins, 1649–1971*. 3rd edn., 1971.

Ruding, Rev. R., *Annals of the Coinage of Great Britain and Its Dependencies*. 1840.

Seaby, H. A. and Rayner, P. A., *The English Silver Coinage from 1649*. 1974.

Seaby, Peter, *The Story of English Coinage*. 1952.

——, *Coins and Tokens of Ireland*. 1970.

Stewart, I., *The Scottish Coinage*. 1976.

Waters, Arthur, *Notes on the Silver Tokens of the Nineteenth Century*. 1957.

Whiting, J. R. S., *Trade Tokens: A Social and Economic History*. 1971.

Whitting, P. D., *Coins in the Classroom*. 1966.

Wright, L. V. W., *Colonial and Commonwealth Coins*. 1966.

Yeoman, R. S., *A Guidebook of United States Coins*. Regularly reprinted.

Publications

Annual Reports of the Deputy Master and Comptroller of the Royal Mint.

British Numismatic Journal, The (British Numismatic Society).

Coin and Medal Bulletin (B. A. Seaby, Ltd., London).

Glendining and Company (London), auction catalogues.

Numismatic Chronicle, The (Royal Numismatic Society).

Numismatic Circular, The (Spink and Son, Ltd., London).

Numismatic Notes and Monographs (The American Numismatic Society).

REFERENCE NOTES

I: Introduction: A Coin of Convenience

1 An interesting discussion of the value of money during the Anglo-Saxon period may be found in Appendix I ("The Anglo-Saxon Government and Manners") of David Hume's *History of England* (Vol. 1) from which several examples have been cited by the author.

2 The purchasing power of the shilling since the Middle Ages has varied according to the rate of inflation, of which some of the sharpest increases have occurred in the present century. Most of the citations from this period are taken from John Burnett's highly readable *A History of the Cost of Living* (Penguin Books, London, 1969).

3 This visit is described in Cobbett's *Rural Rides* originally published in 1830.

4 Apart from the extract quoted, *The Diary of Samuel Pepys* contains several other interesting references to coinage during the period 1659–69.

5 *The Spectator* (essay no. 245, Dec. 11th, 1711).

6 Miss F. Hardcastle kindly provided this example of a shilling's use as gleaned from old records of the village of Burley, Hampshire.

7 I am indebted to Mrs. S. Watney for this nugget of driving wisdom.

8 *Everywoman's Encyclopedia* (n.d.), p. 4077.

9 From a letter to the author from C. N. Popper of The Shilling Coffee Company, Ltd.

10 *Final Report of the Decimal Coinage Commissioners* (London, 1859).

11 *Report of His Majesty's Commissioners* [on Decimal Coinage] (London, 1920).

II: Out of the Dark Came the Shilling

1 For the list of words from which the term "shilling" may be derived, I have resorted to several standard numismatic references plus suggestions by Kenneth Jonsson of the Swedish Royal Mint and Jan H. Nordbø of the University of Oslo.

2 Grierson, Philip, "Notes on Early Tudor Coinage" (*BNJ*, 1971), pp. 80–94.

3 The difficulties in assigning a precise date to Henry VII's testoon are discussed by George C. Brooke (*English Coins*, p. 164) and Sir Charles Oman (*The Coinage of England*, p. 241).

4 Helen Farquhar in "Portraiture of our Tudor Monarchs on Their Coins and Medals," *British Numismatic Journal*, 1908 (p. 90).

5 For an illustrated explanation of how hammered coins were struck see P. D. Whitting's *Coins in the Classroom* (The Historical Association, T.H. 22, 1966), especially p. 15.

6 Sir John Craig, *The Mint*, p. 109.

7 Fabyan's chronicle was first published in 1516; another edition appeared in 1811.

8 W. C. Jordan (editor), *The Chronicle and Political Papers of King Edward VI*, (London: George Allen & Unwin, 1966); entry for April 10th, 1551 (p. 58).

9 Extract from Latimer's sermon as quoted by Rev. Rogers Ruding in *Annals of the Coinage of Britain and its Dependencies*, Vol. II, p. 89.

10 John Taylor (1580–1653), the celebrated water-poet," published an edition of his works in 1630. Another edition, containing more of Taylor's works, was printed by the Spenser Society during 1868–9.

11 From William Shakespeare, "Merry Wives of Windsor," Act I, Scene I.

12 Sir Clement Markham, *King Edward VI*, p. 130, from a sermon by Latimer.

13 For an account of Sharington's misdeeds, see Dr. C. E. Challis' *The Tudor Coinage*, pp. 100–103.

III: Two Queens – and A Bard

1 Samuel Butler, *Hudibras*, in three parts, published in 1663, 1664, and 1668. The couplet is taken from Part III, Canto I, lines 688–9.
2 Helen Farquhar, "Portraiture of Our Tudor Monarchs on Their Coins and Medals," *British Numismatic Journal*, 1908, p. 122.
3 Ben Jonson, "The Alchemist," 1610.
4 George Vertue, *Medals, Coins, Great Seals, Impressions from the Work of Thomas Simon* (London, 1753).

IV: The Early Stuarts and the Amazing Civil War Coinage

1 For an illustrated list of mintmarks·on British coins see Seaby's *Standard Catalogue of British Coins*, issued annually.
2 Oman, p. 302.
3 Martin Llewellin, *Men, Miracles, with Other Poems* (London: 1656), p. 70.
4 This quotation is from a treatise, "Monarchy or No Monarchy in England," by the astrologer, William Lilly (1602–1681). Lilly sided with Charles I during the Civil Wars and in 1651 wrote *True History of King James I and King Charles I*.
5 Butler, *Hudibras*, Pt. 1, Canto 2.
6 Thomas May, *History of the [Long] Parliament* (1647), Vol. II, p. 97.
7 Harold Charles Moffatt, *Old Oxford Plate* (London, 1906), ix.
8 Martin Folkes, *Tables of English Silver and Gold Coins* (London, 1763), p. 87.
9 *ibid.*
10 Moffatt, x–xi.
11 Philip Nelson, *The Obsidional Money of the Great Rebellion* (1907), pp. 11–12.
12 Nelson, p. 9.
13 From original ms. of Sir Hugh Cholmondeley's narrative of the siege of Scarborough (Bodleian Library).
14 *ibid.*
15 *ibid.*

V: The Monarchy Lost – and Restored

1 For additional background on Thomas Simon see "Seal-Maker to King and Commonwealth," *Country Life*, Feb. 17th. 1972.
2 *The Diary of John Evelyn, Esq., F.R.S.* (ed. William Bray), 1818 and many later editions.
3 Oman, p. 329.
4 *ibid.*, p. 331.
5 See also *The English Silver Coinage from 1649* by H. A. Seaby and P. A. Rayner (1949 and later editions), p. 12 and p. 34. "Releive" is the spelling on the coin.

VI: Clipping and the Great Recoinage

1 Lord Macaulay, *The History of England* (London, 1896), Vol. IV, pp. 624–5.
2 *ibid.*, p. 625.
3 *Memoirs and Letters of Mary, Queen of England* (Leipzig, 1886), p. 10.
4 Oman, p. 339.
5 Macaulay, Vol. IV, p. 626.
6 *ibid.*, p. 627.
7 *ibid.*, p. 628.
8 *ibid.*, p. 643.
9 *ibid.*, p. 645.

10 From Edwin and Marion Grew's *The Court of William III*, as quoted by Helen Farquhar in "Portraiture of Our Stuart Monarchs on Their Coins and Medals" (*BNJ*, 1912), p. 122.
11 *The Journeys of Celia Fiennes*, ed., Christopher Morris, (London: The Cresset Press, 1947), p. 78.
12 Samuel Seyer, *Memoirs of Bristol* (II), pp. 544–5.
13 F. Pridmore, "The Officially Pierced Coinage of William III," *Coin and Medal Bulletin* (1949), pp. 573–5.

VII: Enter the Hanoverians

1   Craig, p. 213.
2   Walpole's comments on the Duke and Duchess of Northumberland may be found in his *Memoirs of the Reign of King George III* (4 vols.), first published in 1845.
3   Louis Dutens, *Memoir of a Traveler in Retirement* (c. 1805), pp. 96–8.
4   Walpole, *Memoirs*. See also *Horace Walpole: Memoirs and Portraits* (ed., Matthew Hodgart), 1963, p. 153.
5   Smart's ode appeared on 20 April 1763; his collected poems were published in 1791.
6   The medal collection was sold by Sotheby's on 3 December 1980 and 17 June 1981.
7   Edward Hawkins, *The Silver Coinage of England*, 1887, p. 244.
8   Dutens, pp. 96–8.
9   E. M. Kelly, *Spanish Dollars and Silver Tokens* (London, 1976). p. 7.
10 See also Craig, pp. 261–2 and Oman, p. 358.

VIII: A Silver Token Revolution

1   Oman, p. 362.
2   Kelly, p. 77.
3   Contemporary advertisements and other evidence show that traders sometimes accepted silver tokens issued in towns other than their own.
4   A court in Bath, however ruled that a holder of tokens need not acquire a full pound's worth before they could be redeemed.
5   The concern of citizens of Reading over the banning of the town's silver tokens is described in D. R. D. Edmunds' "The Gold and Silver Tokens Issued by John Berkeley Monck, 1811–1812" (*BNJ*, Vol. XXXV, 1966).
6   Letter to the author from Tom Hanley (Australian Numismatic Society), 25 November 1981.

IX: Token Coinage of the Realm

1   The recoinage of 1816 was an enormous undertaking and has been the subject of many writers. One of the most detailed accounts appears in Sir John Craig's *The Mint*, a work in which an entire chapter (XVI) is devoted to the recoinage.
2   *Annual Report*, The Royal Mint (1966), pp. 6–7.

X: Shillings of an Empress and an Emperor

1   This discounts the short period when Lady Jane Grey was Queen.
2   Craig, p. 298.
3   I am indebted to P. B. Home of Geneva for this anecdote which was passed on to him by his father.
4   See J. E. Hiscott's "Die Numbers on Victorian Coinage" in *Coins* (September, 1972).
5   By contrast, a Silver Jubilee coin was struck for Elizabeth II.
6   Oman, p. 378.

XI: Farewell to the British Shilling

1 For detailed explanations describing the difficulties encountered in preparing the proposed coinage of Edward VIII, I am indebted to Her Majesty's Stationery Office for permission to quote from G. P. Dyer's *The Proposed Coinage of King Edward VIII* (London, 1973).
2 Dyer, p. 3.
3 *ibid.*
4 Dyer, p. 7.
5 Dyer, p. 8.
6 *British Milled Coinage* (List 19), catalogue of Richard Lobel & Co., Ltd., London.

XII: Anglo-Irish and Scottish Shillings

1 For a comprehensive list of Irish coins see *The Guide Book to the Coinage of Ireland* by Anthony Dowle and Patrick Finn (London, 1969), and Peter Seaby's *Coins and Tokens of Ireland* (London, 1970).
2 From a proclamation of James as quoted by Philip Nelson in *The Coinage of Ireland in Copper, Tin, and Pewter* (1905), pp. 71–2.
3 Nelson, p. 3.
4 Nelson, p. 74.
5 Nelson, p. 75.
6 Nelson, pp. 75–6.
7 Scottish silver coins were worth one-fourth English in the reign of Henry VIII, and dropped steadily. By 1601 the Scottish value was only one-twelfth that of the English.

XIII: The Shilling in Other Lands

1 Extract from letters patent as quoted in "The Hog Money of the Somers Islands" by General J. H. Lefroy, *The Numismatic Chronicle & Journal of the Numismatic Society* (1876), pp. 154–5.
2 Letter of instruction to Governor Daniell Tucker (February 15, 1615), par. 25, as quoted by Lefroy, above.
3 Winthrop's journal encompasses the period 1630–49; it was not published until 1825–6. It is regarded as one of the basic documents of early New England history. Published in Boston and edited by James Savage, its title was *The History of New England* (2 vols.)
4 Sylvester S. Crosby, *The Early Coins of America* (Boston, 1875), p. 32.
5 *ibid.*
6 An anonymous American writing in *The Numismatic Magazine*, December, 1902.
7 Letter from Peter Chandler, *Country Life* (July 1, 1971).
8 For a thorough study of the Good Samaritan shilling, see Eric P. Newman's *The Secret of the Good Samaritan Shilling*, Numismatic Notes and Monographs No. 142, The American Numismatic Society (New York, 1959).

XIV: The Shilling in British Custom

1 This account is taken from *Notes and Queries for Somerset and Dorset* (Sherborne, 1931), June (Vol. XX), Note No. 129, pp. 132–3.
2 *Journal of the Society for Army Historical Research* (Vol. 3, 1924), p. 205.
3 *Journal* (Vol. 4, 1925), p. 18.
4 *Manual of Military Law* (1929), p. 215 (note).
5 *Rural Scenes, Or A Peep into the Country for Good Children* (London, 1805).
6 *Notes and Queries* (The Law Society), 3rd S.I., 26 April, 1962, p. 331.
7 *N & Q,* 29 March, 1962, p. 245.

8   *N & Q,* 26 April, 1962, p. 331.
9   E. H. Pearce, *Annals of Christ's Hospital* (1901), pp. 224–5.

XV: The Shilling in Literature and Legend

1   There must be many more proverbs, as well as other references in literature, pertaining to the shilling. The author would be pleased to hear of any others known to readers.

Index